Reach Out

Student Book 1

Ben Wetz

Diana Pye

OXFORD

UNIVERSITY PRESS

▢▢▢▢▢▢▢▢▢ CONTENTS

1 **(● 1.02)** Write the name of objects 1–16 in the picture. Then listen and check.

1 *window*

> board   dictionary   shelf   laptop   clock
> poster   door   ~~window~~   DVD   CD player
> notebook   desk   bag   pen   chair   ruler

2 Look at the picture again and read the sentences. Write *true* or *false*.

The poster is near the door. *false*

1 The DVD is on the shelf.
2 The laptop is next to the DVD.
3 The shelf is near the poster.
4 The poster is under the clock.
5 The notebook is in the bag.
6 The door is between the clock and the board.

3 Write sentences about the picture with the words in the box.

> ~~next to~~   on   on   in   under
> between   near

poster / board
The poster is next to the board.

1 pen / desk   4 pen / notebook
2 ruler / bag   5 board / clock and the
3 CD player / shelf   door
                             6 bag / desk

4 **ACTIVATE** Work in pairs. Say true or false sentences about your classroom. Use the words in the box in exercise 3. Correct your partner's false sentences.

> The window is next to the door.   True.

> The desk is near the board.

> False. The desk is near the windows.

LANGUAGE FOCUS ◼ **Possessive 's and subject and object pronouns** •
Subject pronouns and possessive adjectives
I can talk about people and their possessions.

Possessive 's and subject and object pronouns

1 Translate the phrases. Where's the apostrophe (') in each phrase? Why?

1 David's workbook
2 the teacher's DVDs
3 the boys' bags

2 Write phrases for 1–6. Add an apostrophe (') or 's.

Laura / desk   the students / chairs
Laura's desk   *the students' chairs*
1 David / laptop
2 the teacher / CD player
3 the girl / DVDs
4 Hannah / dictionary
5 William / notebook
6 the students / pens

(More practice ⇨ Workbook page 5)

Subject pronouns and possessive adjectives

3 Complete the table with the words in the box.

his   their   ~~my~~   your   our

Singular		Plural	
Subject pronoun	Possessive adjective	Subject pronoun	Possessive adjective
I	my	we	¹___
you	²___	you	your
he she it	³___ her its	they	⁴___

4 Choose the correct words.

I / My friend Valentina is from Mexico. ¹ **She / Her** last name is Perez. ² **She's / Her** twelve years old. ³ **We're / Our** in class 1B. ⁴ **We / Our** teacher is Michael Adams. ⁵ **His / He's** from Seattle. ⁶ **His / He** English is good. Daniel and Maria are students in ⁷ **my / you** class. ⁸ **They're / Their** thirteen years old.

(More practice ⇨ Workbook page 5)

Object pronouns

5 Match the object pronouns in the box with the subject pronouns.

it   ~~me~~   them   us   you   him   her   you

I – **me**   you – ¹___   it – ²___   he – ³___
she – ⁴___   we – ⁵___   you – ⁶___   they – ⁷___

6 Choose the correct words.

1 That's my desk. Your pen is on **you / it**.
2 Joe and I are here. Tom isn't with **us / them**.
3 Dan is with Sally. Ann is with **her / us**, too.
4 That's Peter. The teacher is with **them / him**.
5 I am here. Amy is with **them / me**.
6 The students are in class. I am not with **you / them**.
7 You and Tom are in class 1B. Joe is with **you / him**.

(More practice ⇨ Workbook page 5)

Checking meaning and spelling

7 🔊 1.03 **Read and listen. Then practice the dialogue.**

Diego How do you say "ventana" in English?
Anna I think it's "window".
Diego Sorry, can you say that again?
Anna Yes, it's "window".
Diego How do you spell that?
Anna W-I-N-D-O-W
Diego Thanks. And what's this in English?
Anna It's a dictionary. Where's your dictionary?
Diego It's in my bag.

8 ACTIVATE Study the key phrases in blue in exercise 7. Then ask and answer questions using the objects in the picture on page 4 or your own ideas.

Reach Out Quiz

Unit 1
This is Sarah's favorite team. Are they good?
1 the U.S. women's national team

Unit 2
It's a big, new building.
2 B__ K__

Unit 4
This is an interesting animal. It's an orca or a ...
4 k__ w__

Unit 6
It's the name of a pizza. Is it a nice name for a girl?
6 M__

Unit 7
He's a popular hero in video games.
7 M__

Unit 3
It's a popular city to live in. People from 179 different countries are here.
3 N__ Y__

Unit 5
Michael is at a very expensive school. It's a ...
5 b__ s__

Unit 8
He's an explorer. His job is difficult, but interesting.
8 K__ F__

---

1 🔊 1.04 Match adjectives 1–7 with their opposites in the box. Then listen and check.

> difficult   unpopular   horrible   small
> ~~bad~~   boring   expensive

1 good   **bad**
2 popular
3 interesting
4 easy
5 big
6 cheap
7 nice

2 Do the *Reach Out* quiz with a partner. Find the answers in the units of this book.

3 Write eight sentences. Use your ideas and the words in the table.

1 *Top Gear is a popular TV program.*

TV program	place	person	game or DVD
popular ✔	big	interesting	expensive
boring	horrible	nice	difficult
good	small	popular	interesting

Days of the week and months

4 🔊 1.05 Put the days of the week in the correct order. Listen and check.

> Friday   ~~Monday~~   Tuesday   Saturday
> Wednesday   Sunday   Thursday

1   Monday

5 Complete the names of the months.

1 J a nua r y   7 _ u _ y
2 F _ brua _ _   8 Au _ us _
3 _ a _ ch   9 _ _ ptemb _ r
4 A _ r _ l   10 Oc _ _ ber
5 Ma _   11 N _ _ emb _ r
6 J _ ne   12 D _ c _ m _ e _

6 ACTIVATE Make true sentences. Then compare with a partner.

1 My birthday is in ___.
2 My friend's birthday is in ___.
3 My favorite month is ___.
4 My favorite day is ___.
5 Today is ___.
6 ___ and ___ are the weekend.

LANGUAGE FOCUS ■ *be*: affirmative, negative, and questions

I can use *really* and *very* to express emphasis.

1 Complete the table with *am*, *is*, *isn't*, *are*, and *aren't*.

Affirmative		Negative	
I 'm / am		I 'm / am not	
He / She / It 's / ¹ __	in this class.	He / She / It is not / ² __	in this class.
We / You / They 're / are		We / You / They are not / ³ __	

Questions		Short answers
⁴ __ I		Yes, I am. / No, I'm not.
Is he / she / it	in this class?	Yes, he / she / it is. / No, he / she / it isn't.
⁵ __ you / we / they		Yes, we / you / they are. / No, we / you / they aren't.

(More practice ⇨ Workbook page 7)

2 Choose the correct words.

1 Laptops **is** / **are** expensive.
2 My dictionary **is** / **are** on the shelf.
3 Your pen and ruler **is** / **are** in your backpack.
4 Madrid **isn't** / **am not** in Peru.
5 The teacher **am** / **is** next to the board.
6 We **isn't** / **aren't** boring students.

3 Write true sentences. Use affirmative and negative forms of *am*, *is*, and *are*.

1 I __ in class now.
2 We __ in America.
3 Our teacher __ from Seattle.
4 My friends __ nice.
5 My notebook __ on my desk.
6 Books __ expensive.
7 I __ fourteen years old.
8 Harry Potter DVDs __ boring.

4 Complete the questions and write your answers. Then ask and answer.

Is this book interesting? **Yes, it is.**
1 __ your friends nice?
2 __ English important?
3 __ CDs expensive?
4 __ your desk new?
5 __ video games boring?
6 __ Barcelona a good soccer club?
7 __ you twelve years old?
8 __ *The Simpsons* a popular program?

5 Study the key phrases. Then complete the sentences with your own ideas.

KEY PHRASES ○ Adding emphasis

New York is a **very** big place.
Marta is a **really** nice teacher.
English isn't a **very** difficult language.

1 __ isn't a very interesting sport.
2 __ and __ are very nice places.
3 __ is a really horrible DVD.
4 __ is a really good program.
5 __ is a very popular CD.
6 __ aren't very cheap.

6 ACTIVATE Compare your sentences in exercise 5 with a partner.

(Golf isn't a very interesting sport.) (No, it isn't.)

1

Your interests

Start thinking

1 Where is Roger Federer from?
2 Where is Brighton?
3 Who is Beyoncé?

Aims

Communication: I can ...

- talk about my hobbies and interests.
- understand a text about people's interests.
- talk about possessions.
- understand people talking about their hobbies and interests.
- ask and answer general knowledge questions.
- greet and introduce people.
- write an e-mail about myself.

Vocabulary

- Free time
- Hobbies and interests

Language focus

- *have / has*: affirmative, negative, and questions
- Prepositions: *about, of, by*
- Interrogative pronouns
- *this, that, these, those*

Reach Out Options

Extra listening and speaking
Identifying people
⇨ Page 88

Curriculum extra
Visual arts: Color
⇨ Page 96

Culture
Young people around the world
⇨ Page 104

Vocabulary puzzles
Free time
⇨ Page 112

VOCABULARY ◼ Free time
I can talk about my hobbies and interests.

1 ⏺ 1.06 Match the words in the box with photos 1–12 on page 9. Then listen and check.

1 photography

> martial arts   chatting on the Internet   sports   art
> computer games   music   ~~photography~~   watching TV
> animals   bike riding   meeting friends   books

> Pronunciation: Syllables ⇨ Workbook page 90

2 Work in pairs. Do the *Your interests, your future* questionnaire on page 9. Is the key correct for you?

> Are you into meeting friends or chatting on the Internet? I like ...

3 ⏺ 1.07 Study the key phrases. Then listen to six sentences. Which key phrases do you hear?

> **KEY PHRASES ◯ Talking about interests**
> I really like ....   I like ....   I don't like ....
> I love ....   I really hate ....
> I'm into ....   I'm not into ....
> I'm interested in ....   I'm not interested in ....

4 Look at the key phrases. Which phrases are affirmative and which are negative?

I really like ... – affirmative

5 Complete the table with the words in exercise 1. Add one more word to each list.

I really like	I like	I don't like	I really hate
photography		bike riding	

6 **ACTIVATE** Talk about your interests with a partner. Use the key phrases and your answers in exercise 5. Then write six sentences.

> I'm not into art.

> Oh, I like art. I really like photography.

> **◯ Finished?**
> Write five sentences about a classmate. Then read them to the class. Can they guess who it is?
> He / She really likes bike riding.
> He / She hates art.

Questionnaire: Your interests, your future

What are your interests? And what's your future?
Choose the best answers and follow the arrows.

Are you into...

START HERE

meeting friends **OR** chatting on the Internet?

sports **OR** art?

bike riding **OR** computer games?

photography **OR** computer games?

martial arts **OR** music?

animals and pets **OR** watching TV?

sports **OR** watching TV?

bike riding **OR** books and comic books?

chatting on the Internet **OR** music?

You aren't an athletic person, but you like learning.
FUTURE: computer expert **OR** TV critic

You're creative and smart.
FUTURE: artist, writer, **OR** pop star

You're active and friendly.
FUTURE: sports star **OR** TV star

My interests

ALEXIA

I love pop music and I have a lot of CDs. My friends are crazy about The Black Eyed Peas, but I can't stand hip-hop. I really like sports, especially volleyball and tennis, but I hate bike riding. One of my interests is art, but I'm not very good at it!

DAVID

I'm into skateboarding and swimming. I'm good at martial arts, especially taekwondo. My friend Steve likes taekwondo, too, but he doesn't have a green belt. We have a computer at home, but I don't really like computer games. I prefer chatting on the Internet. I like books, especially books about animals. I really like animals, but we don't have a pet.

SARAH

I'm interested in sports, especially soccer. I'm a fan of the U.S. women's national team and I have pictures and posters of the team. I'm not crazy about books, but my friend Lily and I love watching TV. Lily has a TV in her room. One of my interests is photography. I don't have a very good camera, but my pictures are really good.

1 Look at the pictures. What do you think Alexia, Sarah, and David are interested in?

2 ◉ 1.08 Read and listen to the texts. Check your answers in exercise 1.

3. Read the texts again and choose the correct answers.
1 Sarah is not into ___
 a soccer. **b** photography. **c** books.
2 Lily has a ___
 a camera. **b** TV.
 c picture of a soccer team.
3 David is good at ___
 a swimming. **b** taekwondo.
 c computer games.
4 David isn't interested in ___
 a computer games. **b** books.
 c swimming.
5 Alexia is into ___
 a hip-hop. **b** bike riding. **c** pop music.
6 Alexia isn't good at ___
 a art. **b** tennis. **c** volleyball.

4 BUILD YOUR VOCABULARY Find these sentences in the text. Then complete the sentences with the words in blue.
1 I'm ___ books.
2 I ___ chatting on the Internet.
3 I really like sports, ___ volleyball and tennis.
4 I'm ___ of the U.S. women's national team.
5 I'm ___ martial arts.
6 I ___ hip-hop.

5 ABOUT YOU Complete the sentences for you. Then compare your answers with a partner.
1 I'm into books, especially books about ___.
2 I'm crazy / not crazy about ___.
3 I'm good / not good at ___.
4 I'm a fan of ___.
5 I'm interested in ___, but I prefer ___.
6 I can't stand ___.

> I'm into books about animals. What about you?

> I prefer comic books.

LANGUAGE FOCUS ◼ *have / has*: **affirmative, negative, and questions** •
Prepositions: *about, of, by*
I can talk about possessions.

1

have

1 Complete the sentences from the text on page 10. Then complete rules 1–5.

I **have** pictures and posters.
Lily ¹___ a TV in her room.
I ²___ a very good camera.
He ³___ a green belt.
We ⁴___ a pet.
We ⁵___ a computer.

> ◯ **RULES**
>
> 1 We use *have* with *you, they,* ___ and ___.
> 2 We use *has* with *she, it* and ___.
> 3 The negative of *have* is ___.
> 4 The negative of *has* is ___.

2 Match the questions with the answers. Then complete the rules.

1 Does she have a TV?
2 Does he have a green belt?
3 Do you have a pet?
4 Do your friends have pets?

a Yes, she does.
b No, they don't.
c No, he doesn't.
d Yes, I do.

> ◯ **RULES**
>
> 1 We make affirmative short answers with *Yes,* + pronoun + *do* / ¹___.
> 2 We make negative short answers with *No,* + pronoun + ²___ / ³___.

(More practice ⇨ Workbook page 9)

3 Complete the sentences. Use *have, has, doesn't have,* or *don't have.*

Tony ___ a pet. ✘
Tony doesn't have a pet.
1 We ___ two dogs. ✔
2 I ___ a poster of Johnny Depp. ✘
3 My mom ___ two cars. ✔
4 She ___ a Ferrari. ✘
5 I ___ a camera. ✔
6 My parents ___ a computer. ✘

4 Write questions. Then ask and answer with a partner.

your friend / laptop?
Does your friend have a laptop? Yes, he does.

1 your teacher / a cell phone?
2 your parents / video camera?
3 you / a bicycle?
4 your school / a soccer team?
5 your friend / a black belt in taekwondo?
6 you / a hobby?

Prepositions: *about, of, by*

5 Work in pairs. Study the examples. Then look at Marta's possessions. Ask and answer about the things she has.

a book / DVD about soccer / Picasso
a picture / poster of London / Roger Federer
a book / CD by J.R.R. Tolkien / Maroon 5

a DVD about animals

> **Does she have a DVD about animals?**   **No, she doesn't.**

1 a picture of London
2 a book about art
3 a book by J.K. Rowling
4 a DVD about skateboarding
5 a CD by Coldplay
6 a poster of a soccer team

(More practice ⇨ Workbook page 9)

6 **ACTIVATE** Ask people in the class about their possessions. Use *about, of,* and *by*, and your own ideas.

> **Do you have a DVD about martial arts?**
>
> **No, I don't. What about you?**

> ◯ *Finished?*
> **Write about your own possessions. Use ideas from exercise 5.**
> **I have a picture of New York.**

1 Complete the mind map with the words in the box.

> ~~hip-hop~~ actor guitar laptop group
> player team e-mail mouse movie
> swimming website classical ~~program~~

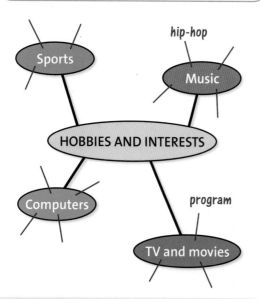

Sports

Music — hip-hop

HOBBIES AND INTERESTS

Computers

TV and movies — program

STUDY STRATEGY ○ Using a mind map

2 Match clues 1–5 with the words in the box. Then add the words to the mind map in exercise 1.

> game drummer ~~science fiction~~
> director singer webcam skiing

a type of movie *science fiction*
1 two words for people in a pop group
2 a popular sport in Switzerland
3 Steven Spielberg is a famous one
4 a camera you use with a computer to show a video on the Internet
5 something that two people or a team play

3 Think of people or things for 1–6.

a hip-hop artist
Rihanna is a hip-hop artist.
1 an American actor
2 a popular TV program
3 a bad movie
4 a boring pop group
5 a good sports team
6 an interesting website

4 🔊 1.09 Read the questionnaire. Then listen to the conversation. Which questions does Rob ask Naomi?

FIND-A-FRIEND QUESTIONNAIRE

ABOUT YOU
1 Where are you from?
2 How old are you?
3 When's your birthday?

YOUR INTERESTS
4 Who are your favorite actors?
5 What's your favorite movie or TV program?
6 Are you good at sports?
7 How many CDs do you have?
8 Who's your favorite sports star?
9 What computer games do you have?
10 Do you have a pet?

5 🔊 1.09 Listen again and write *true* or *false*. Correct the false sentences.

1 Naomi and Rob have birthdays in October and November.
2 Rob is a Keira Knightley fan.
3 Naomi's favorite sports star is a tennis player.
4 Rob is interested in photography.
5 Naomi has a cat.
6 In Naomi's opinion, rats are horrible.

6 ACTIVATE Translate the words in blue in the questionnaire. Then do the questionnaire with a partner.

1   Complete the questions with the words in
the box. Then check your answers in the
questionnaire on page 12.

How many   Who   ~~What~~   When
Where   How old

What's your favorite movie?
1   ___'s your favorite sports star?
2   ___ are you from?
3   ___'s your birthday?
4   ___ are you?
5   ___ CDs do you have?

More practice ⇨ Workbook page 11

2   Complete the questions to match the answers.

When 's lunch? It's at 1:30.
1   ___ DVDs do you have? I have two.
2   ___'s your favorite singer? Rihanna.
3   ___'s your favorite color? Blue.
4   ___'s your dad from? He's from Rome.
5   ___'s your friend's birthday? It's in December.
6   ___ are your parents? They're 38 and 39
years old.

3   Write true answers to the questions in
exercise 2. Then ask and answer in pairs.

How many DVDs do you have?   I have six.

4   ● 1.10   Work in pairs. Complete the quiz
questions and then do the quiz. Listen and
check.

5   **ACTIVATE**   Write one more question about
each topic in the quiz. Use the words in the
box or your own ideas. Then test your partner.

Who / singer / in Coldplay?
Who / Spider-Man?
How many legs / a spider?
When / next soccer World Cup?
Where / Bart Simpson from?
What / Facebook?

INTERESTS QUIZ

Music
1   **Where's** hip-hop music
from?
2   ___'s the singer and ___
does she have in her
hand?

TV and movies

3   What do the letters "MTV"
stand for?
4   ___'s this actor and ___'s
the name of his character
in this movie?

Animals
5   How many eyes
does a spider have?
6   ___'s this animal
and ___'s it from?

Sports
7   ___ and ___ is the
Wimbledon tennis
championship?
8   ___'s this and ___'s his
sport?

Books and comic books
9   ___'s the name of the
famous character in
J.K. Rowling's books?
10   ___'s this and ___ city
is he from?

Computers
11   ___ do the letters
"www" stand for?
12   ___'s the Internet:
50 years or
100 years?

Jake	Hi, Laura. How are things?
Laura	Not bad. How are you, Jake? This is Tina. She's my cousin. She's from the U.K.
Jake	Hello, Tina. Good to meet you.
Tina	And you. Hey, that's a cool T-shirt. Are you into surfing?
Jake	Yes, but I'm not very good. What part of the U.K. are you from?
Tina	I'm from Brighton.
Jake	That's cool. See you later, then.
Tina	Yeah. See you later.

1 Look at the picture. What hobby do you think the boy is interested in? Why?

2 ● 1.11 Listen to the dialogue. Check your answers in exercise 1.

3 ● 1.12 Listen and repeat the key phrases. What are the responses to the key phrases in the dialogue? Practice the dialogue.

> **KEY PHRASES ○ Greeting and introducing people**
>
> 1 How are things?
> 2 This is (Tina).
> 3 Good to meet you.
> 4 Are you into (surfing)?
> 5 What part of (the U.K.) are you from?
> 6 See you later, then.

Language point: *this, that, these, those*

4 Translate the sentences in the table. What's the difference between *this* / *that* and *these* / *those*?

singular	plural
This is my friend.	These are my friends.
That's a good picture.	Those are good pictures.

(More practice ⇨ Workbook page 11)

5 ● 1.13 Look at the picture and complete the dialogue with *this*, *that*, *these*, or *those*. Listen and check. Then practice the dialogue in pairs.

Amy	¹___'s a cool T-shirt.
Ben	Yes. ²___ is my Arsenal shirt. What's ³___?
Amy	⁴___ is my class picture. Hey, are ⁵___ my CDs?
Ben	No, ⁶___ are my Coldplay CDs. ⁷___'s your CD on the table.

6 **ACTIVATE** Work in groups of three. Look at the dialogue in exercise 2. Change the words in blue using the ideas in the box or your own ideas. Practice the new dialogue.

> friend pen pal guitar music picture
> photography Canada Australia
> Toronto Sydney

WRITING ● An e-mail

I can write an e-mail about myself.

○○○

Delete Reply Reply All Forward New Mailboxes Get Mail   Q▾ From   Search Mailbox

Hi,

1   My name's Beth. I'm thirteen years old and I'm a student at Liberty High School in Miami.

2   I like sports, especially basketball and tennis. My favorite tennis player is Rafael Nadal. My friends love soccer, but I hate it. My other interests are music and chatting on the Internet. I'm really into pop music, but I don't have a favorite group.

3   What about you? Do you have any hobbies or interests? Please write and send a picture if you have one.

Bye for now,
Beth

1   Read the model text and answer the questions.

  1 Who is the e-mail to?
    a Beth
    b a student at a different school
    c Beth's sister
  2 What is the purpose of the e-mail?
  3 Is this e-mail formal or informal?
  4 Which paragraph asks the reader questions?
  5 Which paragraph is about Beth's interests?
  6 Which paragraph introduces Beth?

2   Complete the key phrases. Then look at the model text and check.

> **KEY PHRASES ○ E-mail introduction**
>
> 1 I'm a ___ at ….
> 2 I'm ___ into ….
> 3 What ___ you?
> 4 Send a picture if you have ___.
> 5 Bye for ___.

Language point: *and, or, but*

3   Look at the model text. When do we use *and*, *or*, and *but*? Complete the sentences with *and*, *or*, or *but*.

  1 I'm into tennis ___ basketball.
  2 I'm good at tennis, ___ I'm not good at basketball.
  3 Do you prefer dancing ___ photography?
  4 I have a camera, ___ I don't have a laptop.
  5 Is this your book ___ your brother's book?
  6 I really like judo ___ taekwondo.

4   ACTIVATE   Follow the steps in the writing guide.

> **○ WRITING GUIDE**
>
> **A   TASK**
>
> Write an e-mail to Beth about your interests.
>
> **B   THINK AND PLAN**
>
> 1 What's your name and age?
> 2 Where are you from and what's your school?
> 3 What are your hobbies and interests?
> 4 What are your favorite sports, groups, books, or movies?
> 5 Do you have any pets?
> 6 What questions do you have for Beth?
>
> **C   WRITE**
>
> Write your e-mail. Use *and*, *or*, and *but* and the key phrases.
> **Paragraph 1: Introduction**
> *My name's …*
> **Paragraph 2: Hobbies and interests**
> *I'm really into …*
> **Paragraph 3: Questions**
> *What about you?*
>
> **D   CHECK**
>
> • *and*, *or*, and *but*
> • spelling

Vocabulary

1 Find the odd word out in each group.

1 hip-hop classical skiing guitar
2 mouse science fiction webcam laptop
3 bike riding director movie actor
4 swimming website team player
5 drummer group program singer
6 game e-mail taekwondo tennis

2 Complete the sentences with the words in the box.

> can't especially fan good
> crazy prefer

1 I'm not ___ about books.
2 My brother's a Barcelona ___.
3 I like art, but I'm not very ___ at it.
4 We're really into music, ___ hip-hop and pop.
5 I like chatting on the Internet, but I ___ meeting friends.
6 I have a rat, but my mother ___ stand it.

Language focus

3 Write sentences with *have*, *has*, *don't have*, or *doesn't have*.

Tania / a book about art ✗
Tania doesn't have a book about art.
1 My friends / a good computer game ✔
2 Olivia / a poster of the Barcelona team ✔
3 Tim / a black belt in judo ✗
4 We / a CD by The Beatles ✗
5 I / a picture of my class ✔
6 You / a camera ✗
7 Peter / a horrible rat ✔
8 My friends / pets ✗

4 Complete questions 1–6 with the words in the box. Then match the questions with answers a–f.

> When Who What How many
> Where How

1 ___'s your mother from?   a In June.
2 ___ old is your cat?   b Sally Haines.
3 ___'s Steve's birthday?   c Tennis.
4 ___'s your favorite sport?   d Thirty.
5 ___'s your best friend?   e Florida.
6 ___ DVDs do we have?   f Six months old.

5 Look at the pictures and complete the sentences with *this*, *that*, *these*, or *those*.

1 ___ is my favorite book.

2 Is ___ your cat, Tom?

3 ___ are your CDs over there.

4 ___ aren't my comic books.

Communication

6 Match expressions 1–8 with responses a–h.

1 This is Tim.
2 What part of the U.S. are you from?
3 I'm really into music. What about you?
4 Are you into skateboarding?
5 See you later, then.
6 How are things?
7 I hate rats. What about you?
8 Good to meet you.

a Not bad.
b Me too, especially hip-hop.
c I like them, but I prefer cats.
d And you.
e I'm from Boston.
f Yes, but I'm not very good.
g Hello, Tim.
h Yeah. See you later.

Listening

7 🔘 1.14 Listen to four people talking about their interests. Match sentences a–e with speakers 1–4. There is one sentence that you do not need.

Speaker 1		Speaker 3	
Speaker 2		Speaker 4	

a I have a computer.
b I love hip-hop and I'm a Jay-Z fan.
c I'm good at tennis.
d I like playing soccer.
e I really hate rats.

1 Read Sandra's poster. Match the texts with a heading from the box.

Books and comic books   Music   TV and movies   Pets   Name and age   Sports   Computers

1 ___
My name is Sandra. I'm 13 years old. My birthday is in May.

ABOUT ME

4 ___
I'm really into hip-hop, especially The Black Eyed Peas. I play the guitar and I like singing.

2 ___
I have a dog. His name is Scruffy and I love him! I really love animals, especially horses, but I don't have one.

5 ___
We have a computer at home. I use it every day, but I don't like it. I prefer sending text messages with my cell phone.

3 ___
I'm crazy about snowboarding and swimming. I really like basketball, too, but I'm not very good at it.

6 ___
I love reading books. We have a lot of books at home. I'm a big fan of Harry Potter!

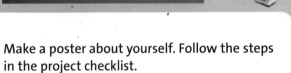
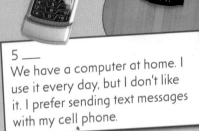

2 Make a poster about yourself. Follow the steps in the project checklist.

7 ___
I really like TV programs about animals or music. I don't like detective movies and I can't stand horror movies.

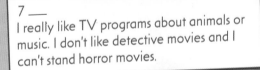

○ **PROJECT CHECKLIST**

1 Find a picture of yourself.
2 Write a few sentences about each of these topics: name and age, pets, sports, music, computers, books and comic books, and TV and movies.
3 Take a big sheet of paper and stick your picture in the middle. Put the texts around it.
4 Put some more pictures or drawings on your poster.

3 Work in groups of five or six. Take one poster and don't let the others see it. Then read one of the texts. Can they guess who it is? If not, read another text.

4 Put all of the posters on the wall. Read the posters and try to find someone with similar interests to yours.

2

City to city

Start thinking

1. Where is the Burj Khalifa?
2. Where is Miami?
3. What is the population of your town or city?

Aims

Communication: I can ...

- describe a town I know.
- understand an article about a city.
- ask and answer questions about my ideal place to live.
- understand descriptions and describe where I live.
- compare places in different countries.
- ask for travel information.
- write about a town or city I like.

Vocabulary

- Places in a town
- Describing places

Language focus

- *there is, there are + a, an, some,* and *any*
- *Is there ...?, Are there ...?*
- Comparative adjectives
- Prepositions: *by* and *on*
- Position of adjectives

Reach Out Options

Extra listening and speaking

Giving personal information

⟹ Page 89

Curriculum extra

Geography: Reading a map

⟹ Page 97

Culture

The United States

⟹ Page 105

Vocabulary puzzles

Places in a town; Describing places

⟹ Page 113

VOCABULARY ■ Places in a town
I can describe a town I know.

1 🔊 1.19 Match twelve of the words in the box with places 1–12 in the *City Simulation* game on page 19. Then listen and check.

1 train station

> ~~train station~~ office building library stores café apartment building art gallery shopping mall hospital park river movie theater community center school restaurant parking lot factory bus station supermarket

2 🔊 1.20 Listen. Where are the people in situations 1–8?

3 🔊 1.21 Work in pairs. Read information A–D in the *City Simulation* game and choose *a* or *b*. Then listen and check.

> I think that "A" is a good place for the ...

Language point: *there is, there are + a, an, some,* and *any*

4 Look at the *City Simulation* game and write *true* or *false* for sentences 1–4. Then complete rules a–c with *a, an, some,* and *any*.

1 There aren't any factories downtown.
2 There are some stores in South Newville.
3 There's a river.
4 There isn't an art gallery.

a We use ___ with plural nouns in affirmative sentences.
b We use ___ with plural nouns in negative sentences.
c We use ___ or ___ with singular nouns in affirmative and negative sentences.

> More practice ⟹ Workbook page 17

5 Complete the sentences about Newville using *There is / isn't, There are / aren't,* and *a / an, some,* and *any*.

There aren't any stores near the school.
1 ___ apartment buildings next to the park.
2 ___ apartment buildings next to the factory.
3 ___ school near the factory.
4 ___ factory near the community center.
5 ___ office buildings in the park.
6 ___ restaurant opposite the shopping mall.

6 **ACTIVATE** Write three true and three false sentences about Newville for your partner. Use the words in exercise 1 and *There's / There are / There isn't / There aren't*. Then correct your partner's false sentences.

> There's a library in the park.

> False. There isn't a library in the park.

City Simulation

A North Newville. There are some factories in this part of the city. We're next to the train station and near downtown. This is a good place for …
a the bus station.
b the library.

B It's opposite the community center. It's also near the Newville shopping mall. There aren't any factories here. There are 10,000 visitors every day. This is a good place for …
a the movie theater.
b the hospital.

C This is downtown, with its fantastic stores and restaurants. Downtown is a good place for …
a the library.
b a new train station.

D South Newville. There are one or two office buildings here, but it's a nice area. It's near a park and there's a river. This is a good place for …
a some factories.
b the hospital.

O *Finished?*
What are the good and bad things about your town or city? Write sentences.
☺ There are two parks.   ☹ There isn't a movie theater.

1 ● 1.22 Look at the pictures and choose six words that you can use to describe the building. Then read, listen, and check your answers.

> elevator   museum   stairs   lake   desert   skyscraper   mountains   modern

City in the sky

Dubai, in the United Arab Emirates, is different from other cities. It is a city of glass skyscrapers in the desert. One of these is the incredible Burj Khalifa skyscraper. It is 828 meters high and has more than 160 floors. You can see it from about 100 kilometers away! The temperature in the desert is sometimes 50°C, but it's cool inside this modern building.

This amazing skyscraper is large enough for 25,000 people. It has a luxury hotel, offices, restaurants, swimming pools, libraries, a gym, and 900 expensive apartments. From the visitor area on the 124th floor, the cars in the street below are tiny. The tower has 57 very fast elevators, but there are also lots of stairs if you have lots of energy!

In the Burj Khalifa area, there are parks and a large lake. There is a big shopping mall next to the tower.

This enormous building has over 1,200 luxury stores. The city of Dubai is a fantastic place, but only if you are very rich and you like shopping.

2 Read the text again and write *true* or *false*. Correct the false sentences.

1 The Burj Khalifa skyscraper is 100 km away from Dubai.
2 The skyscraper is a very old building.
3 There are 800 apartments in the skyscraper.
4 There is a place for visitors on floor 124.
5 The elevators in the tower are pretty slow.

STUDY STRATEGY ○ **Finding spelling rules**

3 Find the plural forms of these words in the text. When do we form a plural with *-ies*?

> office   city   apartment   park   store   library

4 **BUILD YOUR VOCABULARY** What do these adjectives describe? Find them in the text and check.

> amazing   luxury   enormous   incredible   fantastic   tiny   fast

5 **ABOUT YOU** Ask and answer the questions.

1 Is the Burj Khalifa a good place to live?
2 Why is the Burj Khalifa only good for rich people?
3 Are there any interesting buildings in your town?
4 Is there a shopping mall in your town?
5 How many parks are there?
6 What are your favorite places?

LANGUAGE FOCUS ◻ *Is there … ?, Are there … ?*
I can ask and answer questions about my ideal place to live.

2

1 Complete the questions from exercise 5 on page 20. Then match the questions with the answers a–c.

Are there ¹___ interesting buildings?
How many parks ²___ there?
³___ there a shopping mall?

a Three.
b Yes, there are.
c No, there isn't.

2 Choose the correct answers.

> ◻ **RULES**
>
> 1 We use *some* / *any* in questions.
> 2 We use *Yes, there is* and *No, there isn't* with **singular nouns** / **plural nouns**.
> 3 We use *Yes, there are* and *No, there aren't* with **singular nouns** / **plural nouns**.

(More practice ⟹ Workbook page 17)

3 Complete the questions with *Is there* / *Are there*. Then ask and answer with a partner. Give short answers.

1 ___ a park or garden in your town?
2 ___ any old buildings in your town?
3 ___ any mountains near your town?
4 ___ a river in your town?
5 ___ any places for young people where you live?
6 ___ any stores near your school?
7 How many restaurants ___ in your town?
8 How many houses ___ in your street?

(Is there a park or garden in your town?)

(Yes, there is.)

4 Put the key phrases in order.

no ___ ___ ___ lots (of)

> **KEY PHRASES** ◯ **Expressing quantity**
>
> only one   lots (of)   one or two
> a lot of   no

5 Think about your ideal place to live. Is it a big city or a small town? Write six sentences with *There is … / There are …* and the key phrases in exercise 4. Use the phrases in the box and your own ideas.

In my ideal place to live there are no factories.

> a big shopping mall   a skateboard park
> schools   factories   old buildings
> tall buildings   a river   a park
> big forests   hospitals

6 **ACTIVATE** Ask your partner about their ideal place to live. How many of your ideas are the same? Use *Is there … ?, Are there … ?,* and *How many … ?* and your own ideas in exercise 5. Give short answers.

(My ideal place to live is a small town.)

(Is there a skateboard park in your ideal town?)

(Yes, there is.)

> ◯ *Finished?*
> **Write a description of your ideal place to live. Use your ideas in exercise 5 and adjectives from page 20.**
> There are lots of tiny stores.
> There are one or two fantastic restaurants.

1 🔊 1.23 Match adjectives 1–6 with their opposites. Then listen and check.

> quiet dirty safe unfriendly pretty modern

1 dangerous ___

2 friendly ___

3 noisy ___

4 clean ___

5 ugly ___

6 old ___

2 Complete the sentences about where you live. Use the adjectives in exercise 1. Then compare your sentences with a partner.

My city is very **modern**.
1 The streets are very ___.
2 The buildings are really ___.
3 The people are really ___.
4 The houses are ___.
5 The downtown area is ___.
6 The country around the city is ___.

3 🔊 1.24 Jake is from Miami and Tina is from Brighton. Listen to their conversation. Which city does Tina prefer? Why?

Miami

Brighton

4 🔊 1.24 Listen again and write *true* or *false*.

1 Miami is bigger than Brighton.
2 Miami is safer than Brighton.
3 Brighton is a prettier place.
4 Brighton is more exciting than Miami.
5 The people in Miami are friendlier.
6 The weather is better in Brighton.

5 ACTIVATE Think of a town or city in your country. Don't tell your partner. Then ask your partner questions using adjectives in exercise 1 and guess their town or city.

Is it a noisy city?

No, it's a very quiet city.

Are there a lot of modern buildings?

No, there aren't. The buildings are very old.

LANGUAGE FOCUS ■ Comparative adjectives
I can compare places in different countries.

2

1 Complete the table with adjectives in exercise 4 on page 22. How do you make comparatives in your language?

	Adjective	Comparative
Short adjectives and adjectives ending in -y	old safe big pretty friendly	older 1 ___ 2 ___ 3 ___ 4 ___
Long adjectives	dangerous exciting	more dangerous 5 ___
Irregular adjectives	bad good far	worse 6 ___ further

More practice ⟹ Workbook page 19

2 ● 1.25 Complete the sentences. Do the quiz with a partner. Then listen and check. Is the word *than* before or after the adjective in comparative sentences?

All around the world

1 Tokyo is ___ (expensive) than Rome.   True / False

2 New York is ___ (new) than Athens.   True / False

3 The Atlantic is ___ (wide) than the Pacific.   True / False

4 Everest is ___ (high) than Mont Blanc.   True / False

5 The Rhine is ___ (long) than the Amazon.   True / False

6 Cape Town is ___ (dangerous) than Zurich.   True / False

7 Mexico City is ___ (old) than Venice.   True / False

8 Paris is ___ (far) than Madrid from London.   True / False

3 Write six more sentences for the quiz using these words or your own ideas. Then test your partner.

> The weather in Italy is worse than here.

> No. The weather in Italy is better than here.

1 weather in Italy / weather here (bad / good)
2 Brazil / Canada (cold / hot)
3 the Danube / the Nile (short / long)
4 Australia / Poland (big / small)
5 the Andes / the Alps (high / low)
6 Prague / Los Angeles (new / old)

4 Look at the table. Write questions with comparative adjectives and *than*. Then ask and answer with a partner.

> Is Oldington older than Newville?

> Yes, it is.

	Newville	Oldington
old	10 years	600 years
friendly	☺ ☺ ☺	☺ ☺
safe	☺ ☺	☺ ☺ ☺
quiet	✔ ✔	✔ ✔ ✔
interesting	✔ ✔	✔ ✔ ✔ ✔
ugly	✔ ✔	✔

Pronunciation: /ə/ ⟹ Workbook page 90

5 Look at the pictures of Mexico City and Unalaska. Write your opinions about the cities.

I think that the weather is worse in Unalaska.

1 the weather / bad
2 the air / clean
3 life / exciting
4 the streets / dangerous
5 country / beautiful
6 the people / friendly

Mexico City, Mexico

Unalaska, U.S.

6 ACTIVATE Compare two cities with a partner using words in exercise 5 and your own ideas.

> The weather in São Paulo is worse than in Rio de Janeiro.

> Life in Salvador is more exciting than in Brasília.

🔲 *Finished?*
Compare your town or city to Mexico City and Unalaska. Write five sentences.
My town is smaller than Mexico City.

Man Hello. Can I help you?

Tina Yes, I want to visit Orlando. How far is it from here?

Man Orlando's about ¹___ minutes from here by plane.

Tina OK. How much is a round-trip ticket?

Man A round-trip ticket is ²___ dollars.

Tina And is there a bus or train to Orlando?

Man Yes, there are buses from ³___. They're cheaper than the plane. The schedules are here.

Tina Great. Thanks very much.

1 Look at the picture. Where are the people? What information does Tina want?

2 ⏺ 1.26 Listen and complete the dialogue. How far is Orlando? Which is more expensive, the plane or the bus?

3 Cover the dialogue and complete these key phrases. Practice the dialogue.

> **KEY PHRASES ⭕ Asking for travel information**
>
> 1 I ___ to visit (Orlando).
> 2 How ___ is it from here?
> 3 (Orlando's) about (fifty-five) minutes ___ here.
> 4 How ___ is a one-way / round-trip ticket?

Language point: Prepositions: *by* and *on*

4 Translate the phrases. Do you use the same prepositions in your own language?

by bus / car / train / plane
on the bus / train / plane
on foot

(More practice ⟹ Workbook page 19)

5 Study the examples with *by* and *on* in exercise 4. Ask and answer questions about how far places 1–8 are from here.

(How far is your house from here?)

(It's about ten minutes on foot.)

1 your house
2 Miami
3 the library
4 downtown
5 the next town
6 the beach
7 Argentina
8 the bus station

6 **ACTIVATE** Work in pairs. Prepare a new dialogue using the dialogue in exercise 1 as a model. Change the words in blue using information about your area. Practice the new dialogue.

WRITING ■ A description of a town
I can write about a town or city I like.

2

MY CITY: MIAMI

1   Miami is a city in the south of the United States. It has a population of about 400,000 and there is a lot of tourism here.

2   I like Miami because it's a friendly place and it's very pretty. There are some really old buildings and it has some beautiful parks. For tourists there are a lot of interesting stores and some very good restaurants. My favorite places are the beach and the zoo.

3   Miami is 326 kilometers from Orlando. It's about an hour on the plane, and there are planes and buses from Orlando International Airport.

1 Read the model text and answer the questions.

1   Does the writer like Miami?
2   Which paragraph says how to get to Miami?
3   Which paragraph describes the writer's favorite places?
4   Which paragraph says how many people live in Miami?
5   How is Miami different from your city?

2 Complete the key phrases with the words in the box. Look at the model text and check.

> 400,000   the United States   friendly
> 326   Orlando   the beach and the zoo

KEY PHRASES ○ Describing a town / city

1   It's in the north / south / east / west of ___.
2   It has a population of about ___.
3   It's a ___place.
4   My favorite places are ___.
5   It's ___ kilometers from ___.

3 Use the key phrases to write sentences about your city.

Language point: Position of adjectives

4 Look at the words in blue in the model text. Then choose the correct words in the rules.

○ RULES

1   The adjectives are **before** / **after** the nouns.
2   *Really* and *very* are **before** / **after** the adjectives.

5 Order the words to make sentences.

is / a / very / Paris / city / beautiful
Paris is a very beautiful city.

1   is / big / Los Angeles / city / a
2   exciting / I / places / like
3   safe / are / streets / very / the
4   quiet / is / library / the / building / very / a
5   really / there / some / interesting / are / stores
6   the / has / city / a / park / big

6   ACTIVATE   Follow the steps in the writing guide.

○ WRITING GUIDE

A TASK

Write about a town or city you like.

B THINK AND PLAN

1   Where is the town / city? How big is it?
2   Is there a lot of tourism?
3   Why do you like the town / city?
4   What are your favorite places?
5   Are there any buses, trains, or planes from other places?

C WRITE

Paragraph 1: Location
... is a town / city in ...
Paragraph 2: Good things
... is a great place. I like it because ...
Paragraph 3: Transportation and other places
... is about ... kilometers from ...

D CHECK

• position of adjectives
• position of *very* and *really*
• *there is, there are*

Vocabulary

1 Match the words in the box with the sentences.

> library   bus station   store   park
> community center   restaurant
> movie theater   hospital

1 How much is a round-trip ticket to Orlando?
2 There are some books about art.
3 There's a good movie on tonight.
4 This is a good place for basketball.
5 The food here is very expensive.
6 There are lots of doctors and nurses.
7 It's very nice near the lake.
8 These T-shirts are very cheap.

2 Write the opposites. There are two adjectives that you do not need.

> dangerous   small   unfriendly   ugly
> far   enormous   dirty   exciting
> quiet   old

1 pretty   ___   5 friendly   ___
2 safe   ___   6 modern   ___
3 noisy   ___   7 clean   ___
4 tiny   ___   8 near   ___

Language focus

3 Write affirmative and negative sentences. Use *There's*, *There isn't*, *There are*, or *There aren't*.

a big hospital ✔
There's a big hospital.

1 some factories ✔
2 any office buildings ✘
3 one or two cheap stores ✔
4 a community center ✘
5 any good restaurants ✘
6 a train station ✔
7 a nice library ✔
8 two movie theaters ✔

4 Write questions for the answers in exercise 3. Use *Is there ...?*, *Are there ...?*, and *How many ...?* Then write short answers.

> *Is there a big hospital?*   *Yes, there is.*

5 Complete the sentences with comparative adjectives.

1 This town is ___ (big) than my town.
2 The downtown area is ___ (safe) in the daytime.
3 The city is ___ (exciting) than my town.
4 The weather is ___ (good) in the south of the country.
5 The people here are ___ (unfriendly) than at home.
6 The modern buildings are ___ (tall) than the old ones.

Communication

6 Complete the dialogue with the phrases in the box.

> a lot of   round-trip ticket   How far
> expensive   about   to visit   there's
> by plane

Tom   I want ¹___ Boston.
Lisa   Good idea. I think there are ²___ interesting things to see there.
Tom   Yes, ³___ Fenway Park, the famous baseball stadium.
Lisa   ⁴___ is it from here?
Tom   It's ⁵___ four hours by train.
Lisa   How much is a ⁶___?
Tom   A round-trip ticket is $150.
Lisa   That's very ⁷___. Is it cheaper ⁸___?
Tom   No, it's more expensive.

Listening

7 🔊 1.27 Listen to a description of the city of Charleston and write *true* or *false*.

1 Charleston is in the southeast part of the United States.
2 There are about 650,000 people in Charleston.
3 Charleston has a lot of tall houses.
4 It has a lot of interesting museums.
5 It's about four hours from Washington, D.C. on the plane.
6 A round-trip ticket on the plane is about $250.

Listening

1 Look at the pictures. Answer the questions.

1 Where are the people in picture 1?
2 Who is a basketball player?
3 Who has a camera?

2 🔘 1.28 Listen to a conversation. What are Jon, Lucy, and Tim interested in?

3 🔘 1.28 Listen again and complete the sentences.

1 ___ is from Australia.
2 ___ is crazy about basketball.
3 Lucy is better than ___ at basketball.
4 ___ is into tennis.
5 Darwin is in the ___ of Australia.
6 It's ___ than Sydney.
7 There are a lot of new ___ in Darwin.
8 Jon doesn't have any ___ of Darwin.

Speaking

4 Work in groups of three and prepare a conversation. Imagine that one person is from a different country. Answer the questions.

1 What are your interests?
2 What are you good at?
3 Who is from a different country?
4 Where is he / she from in this country?
5 What is the place like?

5 Have a conversation. Use your ideas in exercise 4 and the chart below to help you. One of you is A, one of you is B and one of you is C. When you have finished, change roles.

A *Hi! How are things?*

B Reply.

A Introduce your friend.
This is ... .
He / She's from ... .

B Reply.

C Reply and ask about B's interests.
Are you into ... ?

B Reply and ask about C's interests.
What about you?

C Reply.

B Ask where C is from.
What part of ... from?

C Reply.

B *Where's that?*

C *It's north / south etc. of ... .*

B *Is it a nice place?*

C Reply.

Writing

6 Write an e-mail to a friend. Tell your friend about a person from a different country. You can write about Jon from the listening activity or another person. Use the sentences in exercise 3 to help you. Begin like this:

Hi ... ,

I have a new friend! His / Her name's ...

He / She's from ...

3

Around the world

Start thinking

1 What's the word for *hello* in Japanese?
2 What is the population of New York City?
3 What is child labor? Where is it a problem?

Aims

Communication: I can ...

- talk about countries, nationalities, and languages.
- understand an article about people living in New York.
- use the simple present to talk about facts and routines.
- talk about daily routines.
- ask people about their routines and habits.
- talk about things I like and don't like doing.
- write a report about a country.

Vocabulary

- Countries, nationalities, and languages
- Routines

Language focus

- Simple present: affirmative and negative
- Adverbs of frequency
- Simple present: questions
- Punctuation

Reach Out Options

Extra listening and speaking
Talking about schedules
⇨ Page 90

Curriculum extra
Language and literature: Non-verbal language
⇨ Page 98

Culture
The English-speaking world
⇨ Page 106

Vocabulary puzzles
Countries and nationalities; Routines
⇨ Page 114

VOCABULARY ■ Countries, nationalities, and languages

I can talk about countries, nationalities, and languages.

1 🔊 1.34 Do the *Go global!* quiz on page 29. Then listen and check your answers.

2 Look at the quiz and write countries for nationalities 1–12 below.

1 Canadian – Canada

1 Canadian	4 British	7 Spanish	10 Chinese
2 American	5 German	8 Polish	11 Japanese
3 Brazilian	6 French	9 Italian	12 Australian

3 Study the key phrases. Which phrase is very certain?

> **KEY PHRASES ○ Guessing answers**
>
> I think it's …. I'm not sure. I don't think it's ….
> Maybe / Perhaps it's …. I'm sure it's ….

4 🔊 1.35 Listen to people from six different countries. Work in pairs. Say what the languages are. Use the key phrases in exercise 3.

> German Spanish Italian French English Mandarin

> I think it's Mandarin.

> I'm not sure. Maybe it's Italian.

5 Make more quiz questions. Then ask and answer using the key phrases in exercise 3.

1 What's the capital of ___?
2 What's the official language of ___?
3 What's the currency in ___?
4 What's the word for ___ in ___?
5 How many countries does ___ have borders with?

6 **ACTIVATE** Write five true and false sentences about countries and languages using the phrases below and your own ideas. Then listen to your partner's sentences. Say if they are true or false using the key phrases in exercise 3.

1 The capital of ___ is ___.
2 The official language of ___ is ___.
3 The currency in ___ is ___.
4 The word for ___ in ___ is ___.
5 ___ has borders with ___.

> The capital of Canada is Montreal.

> I'm not sure. False. I don't think it's Montreal.

> False. I think it's Ottawa.

> **○ Finished?**
>
> Think of a person or thing from six countries.
>
> > city food / dish celebrity word car product
>
> A city in Canada – Toronto A Chinese dish – Chop Suey

Quiz: Go global!

1 Bonjour! In Canada, they speak French and which other language?

2 Hi! Where's the home of the President of the U.S.?

3 Bom dia! We love sports here. What's the national sport of Brazil?

4 Hello! What's the currency in the United Kingdom?

5 Guten Tag! What's the name of the biggest river in Germany, the Rhine or the Rhone?

6 Salut! The population of France is 30 million. True or false?

7 Hola! How many official languages are there in Spain?

8 Dzień dobry! Poland has borders with three countries. True or false?

9 Ciao! What's the word for "pizza" in Italian?

10 Ni hao! People in China don't speak Chinese. Is the main language Mandarin or Beijing?

11 Konichiwa! More than 13 million people live in the capital of Japan. What's its name?

12 G'day! Are there more people in Australia or in Italy?

1 What do you know about New York?

2 ⏺ 1.36 Read and listen to the text. How many languages are mentioned in the text?

3 Read the text again. Choose the correct answers.

1 There are people in New York from ___ in the world.
   a every country **b** 179 countries
   c thirty countries
2 Marcia studies ___ at school.
   a German **b** Mandarin **c** French
3 ___ doesn't speak English fluently.
   a Ana's Mandarin teacher
   b Marcia's French teacher **c** Marcia
4 Damini is ___
   a Turkish. **b** Nigerian. **c** Indian.
5 The text is mainly about ___
   a the languages students learn at school.
   b the different stores in New York.
   c the languages people speak in New York.

4 BUILD YOUR VOCABULARY Find the plural forms of these words in the text. Which one is irregular?

1 person   5 student
2 country   6 word
3 nationality 7 family
4 class   8 store

5 ABOUT YOU Ask and answer the questions.

1 Are there people from different countries in your city?
2 What languages are popular at your school? Why?
3 What countries do you want to visit? Why? Use the ideas below.

> music food movies scenery places
> culture sports

> **▢ Glossary**
> nation: country
> cosmopolitan: including people and things from many different countries and cultures

New York: the world in one city

New York is a very cosmopolitan city. There are people from nearly every nation, culture, and religion in the world. In fact, thirty-six percent of New York's population of 8.2 million comes from outside the U.S. That's about three million people from 179 different countries. Marcia and Damini are two of those people.

Marcia
My parents are from the Dominican Republic and we live in New York. My sister Ana and I go to a school with students from twenty-five different countries. There are classes here in French, German, Spanish, and Mandarin, and I do French. My sister studies Mandarin, with Mrs. Li Wei. Mrs. Wei is a new teacher from Beijing. She doesn't speak English fluently and my sister sometimes helps her with new words.

Damini
I live in a part of New York where there are families of a lot of different nationalities. On my street, there are Mexican and Chinese stores and a Haitian restaurant. My family is from India. My best friend Leyla is from a Turkish family, but they don't speak Turkish at home. We often play music at her house. I like Turkish music because it's different from our music.

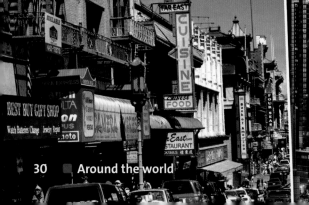

LANGUAGE FOCUS ■ Simple present: affirmative and negative

I can use the simple present to talk about facts and routines.

3

1 Complete the examples from the text on page 30. Then choose the correct answers in rules 1–3.

We **live** in New York.
I ¹___ Turkish music.
My sister ²___ Mandarin.
They ³___ Turkish at home.
She ⁴___ English fluently.
My sister sometimes ⁵___ her with new words.

◯ RULES

1 We use the simple present to talk about **facts and routines / things happening now**.
2 We add -*s* to the *he / she / it* forms in **negative / affirmative** sentences.
3 We use *doesn't / don't / isn't / aren't* to make negative sentences.

(More practice ⇨ Workbook page 25)

2 Check the meaning of the verbs below. Then study the spelling rules and put the verbs in groups 1–3. Which verb doesn't go in any group?

use go have write mix try
carry finish listen eat know sleep
watch buy come teach do make
walk think

◯ SPELLING RULES

1 Most verbs → add -*s* e.g. *use* + -*s* = *uses*
2 Verbs ending in *o, x, ss, ch, sh* → add -*es*
  e.g. *go* + -*es* = *goes*
3 Verbs ending in consonant + -*y* → minus -*y* and add -*ies* e.g. *study* − *y* + -*ies* = *studies*

Pronunciation: Third person singular
⇨ Workbook page 90 and 91

3 Use the verbs in parentheses and write true sentences in the simple present.

1 My father ___ to work every day. (go)
2 My mother ___ French. (teach)
3 At my school, they ___ Mandarin. (do)
4 My friend and I ___ TV every day. (watch)
5 I ___ to learn ten new words every day. (try)
6 The English teacher ___ difficult words on the board. (write)
7 I ___ math. (like)
8 My friends ___ computer games. (play)

4 Complete the text with the correct simple present form of the verbs in the box.

not speak do eat watch ~~come~~
not understand make go live

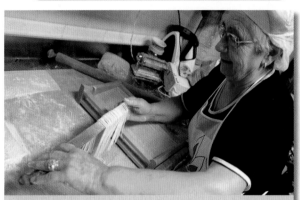

I live in New York, but my family **comes** from Italy. We ¹___ English at home because my grandmother ²___ with us and she ³___ English. She ⁴___ Italian movies all day. My grandmother ⁵___ the cooking at home and she ⁶___ spaghetti every day! When she ⁷___ to Italy in the summer, we ⁸___ hamburgers and French fries every day!

5 **ACTIVATE** Write true and false sentences about yourself. Use affirmative and negative forms of the verbs. Then listen to your partner's sentences. Say if they are true or false.

I read English comic books.
My parents don't eat Japanese food.

like	Italian	cars
watch	French	food
read	Japanese	books / comic books
go to	Spanish	movies / TV programs
eat	English	music
	American	classes

(*I read English comic books.*)

(*I think that's false. I'm sure you don't read English comic books.*)

◯ *Finished?*

Write five true sentences about your partner.
He likes American movies. He doesn't read English comic books.

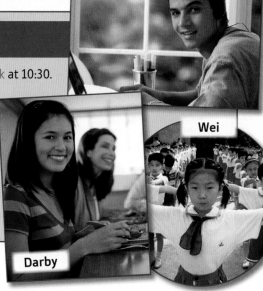

Brad

Wei

My day

Before school we do exercises. We have a break at 10:30.
I have lunch in the classroom at 12 o'clock.
I watch TV before dinner.
I do my homework after dinner.
I go to bed before 9 o'clock.
I get up at 5:30 and then I have breakfast.
I don't go to school. I study at home.
I don't go home. I live where I work.
I have dinner with my family at about 8 o'clock.

Sharif

Darby

1 Check the meaning of the verbs in blue. Put the verbs in the correct order of the day.

get up ...

2 How is your day different from the routines in exercise 1? Make sentences.

STUDY STRATEGY ◯ Predicting

3 ◉ 1.37 Look at the information. Which sentences in exercise 1 do you think are about Sharif? Listen to a radio program about child labor and check your answers.

Sharif's day

Approximately 158 million children aged from five to fourteen work and they don't go to school. Today's program looks at the problem of child labor and the story of Sharif.

Language point: Adverbs of frequency

4 ◉ 1.37 Listen again and complete the text.

In many parts of the world, children work in difficult conditions. They are sometimes only five or six years old. Sharif lives in Bangladesh and he is ¹___ years old. He always gets up at ²___ because he starts work at 6:00 in the morning. He works in a shoe ³___ and he usually works ⁴___ days a week. He often has a lunch break for ⁵___ minutes and he always eats in the street. He is always very tired at the end of the day. He never goes home in the evening. He usually ⁶___ in the factory. His parents live in a different town.

5 Complete the chart with the words in blue in exercise 4. Then choose the correct words in the rules.

0%				100%
never	1 ___	2 ___	3 ___	4 ___

◯ RULES

Adverbs of frequency come ...
1 before / after the verb be.
2 before / after other verbs.

(More practice ⟹ Workbook page 27)

6 Rewrite the sentences so they are true for you. Use adverbs of frequency.

My friends and I do our homework on the bus.
My friends and I never do our homework on the bus.
1 My friend has dinner at eight o'clock.
2 I watch TV after dinner.
3 I'm late for school.
4 We start school at nine o'clock.
5 I get up at six o'clock.
6 We have breakfast at school.
7 I go to bed after midnight.
8 We finish school at four o'clock.

7 ACTIVATE Work in pairs. Compare your sentences in exercise 6.

My friend sometimes has dinner at eight o'clock.

My friend never has dinner at eight o'clock.

I can ask people about their routines and habits.

1 Match questions 1–5 with the answers a–e. Then choose the correct answers in rules 1–3.

1 Does Sharif live with his parents?
2 Do you work in a factory?
3 Does Sara go to school?
4 Do the children eat in the street?
5 Where does Sharif sleep?

a Yes, they do.
b In the factory.
c Yes, she does.
d No, I don't.
e No, he doesn't.

○ RULES

1 We use *do*/*does* / *are*/*is* to make questions.
2 We **add** / **don't add** -s to the *he*/*she*/*it* forms in questions.
3 We put the question word (*where, what, who*, etc.) at the **beginning** / **end** of the question.

(More practice ⇨ Workbook page 27)

2 Write questions and short answers. Then ask and answer with a partner.

you / get up at 5:30

(Do you get up at 5:30?) (No, I don't.)

1 your parents / play tennis
2 your mother / speak Spanish
3 you / watch TV every evening
4 this book / teach vocabulary
5 your father / work in a factory
6 you and your friends / go to school on Saturdays
7 you and your family / live in a modern building
8 your friend / come to your home after school

3 Complete the questions. Then match questions 1–7 with answers a–h.

What time *do you get up* (you / get up) on Sunday? *d*
1 Where ___ (you and your family / go) in the summer?
2 Where ___ (your best friend / live)?
3 When ___ (you / play) sports?
4 How ___ (you / travel) to school?
5 What movies ___ (your friends / like)?
6 How often ___ (you / watch) TV?
7 What ___ (you / do) in the evening?

a I walk.
b Science fiction.
c I watch it every evening.
d At half past nine.
e I watch TV and read.
f I play them on the weekend.
g In New York.
h We go to the beach.

4 Work in pairs. Ask and answer the questions in exercise 3. Give true answers.

(What time do you get up on Sunday?)

(I get up at eleven o'clock.)

5 Write eight questions to find out about people's routines and habits. Use the words below and your own ideas.

What do you do on your birthday?
How often do you have lunch at school?

What	visit	in the summer
Who	go	on the weekend
When	have	lunch
Where	do	in the evening
How often	watch	TV programs
How	get up	late
What time	read	on your birthday
	like	after school

6 **ACTIVATE** Find out about people's routines and habits. Work in groups and ask and answer your questions in exercise 5.

(What TV programs do you like?)

(I like sports programs.)

(Where do you go in the summer?)

(I go to Rio de Janeiro with my family.)

○ *Finished?*
Imagine you can interview your favorite celebrity. Write six questions for your interview. Make up their answers.
Where do you go on vacation in the winter?
I go skiing in the Rocky Mountains.

Amelia Do you play a musical instrument?
Grace Yes, I play the trumpet. I have band practice after school.
Amelia Wow! ¹___
Grace It's great. I really enjoy playing Cuban music, especially the salsa.
Amelia I love dancing salsa. ²___
Ryan I don't mind listening to music, but I hate dancing. I prefer sports.
Amelia What's your favorite sport?
Ryan Baseball. I'm a Yankees fan.
Grace ³___
Ryan Yes, and I like playing it. What do you like doing, Amelia?
Amelia ⁴___ I'm in a pop group at home.
Grace Fantastic! We need a singer in our group.

1 Answer the questions with a partner.

1 Do you play a musical instrument?
2 Do you prefer listening to music, dancing, or playing sports?

2 ⊙ 1.38 Complete the dialogue with a–d. Then listen and check.

a I enjoy singing.
b Ryan likes watching baseball on TV!
c Do you like playing the trumpet?
d What about you, Ryan?

3 Complete the key phrases from the dialogue. Then practice the dialogue.

KEY PHRASES ○ Likes and dislikes

1 I really enjoy ___.
2 I hate ___.
3 (Ryan) likes ___!
4 What do you like doing?
5 Do you like ___?
6 ___ about you, (Ryan)?
7 I don't mind ___.

4 Ask and answer questions with a partner using the activities in the box and the key phrases in exercise 3.

get up early / late   eat chocolate / pizza
watch TV / DVDs   read comic books / books
play tennis / baseball   sing / dance
listen to classical / pop music

Do you like getting up early?   *No, I don't.*

What do you like doing?

I really enjoy playing tennis.

5 ⊙ 1.39 Listen and complete the dialogue.

Girl What do you like doing in the evenings?
Boy I love ¹___. What about you?
Girl I really enjoy ²___.
Boy I don't. I hate reading comic books.
Girl Do you enjoy ³___?
Boy No, but I love listening to pop music.
Girl What do you like doing on the weekend?
Boy I really like ⁴___.
Girl Oh, I don't. I love playing baseball.

6 ACTIVATE Work in pairs. Prepare a new dialogue about likes and dislikes using the dialogue in exercise 5 as a model. Change the words in blue and the answers from the listening. Use the activities in exercise 4 or your own ideas. Practice the new dialogue.

WRITING ■ Country and language report
I can write a report about a country.

3

1 Read the model text and match the paragraphs 1–3 with these topics.

> Languages   Population   Where it is

2 Answer the questions.

1 What nationality and languages are in the report?
2 What is the population of Canada?
3 What languages do people study in Canadian schools?
4 What is the capital city?
5 Which other parts of the world do a lot of people in Canada come from?

3 Look at the model text and complete the key phrases. Then write similar sentences for your country.

> **KEY PHRASES ○ Country fact-file**
>
> 1 It has ___ the (United States) in the (south).
> 2 The ___ is to the ___ of (Canada).
> 3 Most (Canadians) ___ (English).
> 4 (French) is the ___ language in ___.
> 5 A lot of ___ from other countries live ___.
> 6 In particular, there are ___ people from ___.

Language point: Punctuation

4 Read the rules and look at the example sentences. Then find more examples in the model text.

> **○ RULES**
>
> 1 We use capital letters at the beginning of a sentence, with names, countries, nationalities, and languages.
>   *Canada is a large country in North America.*
> 2 We use commas in lists and for pauses.
>   *... but people also study Spanish, German, and Mandarin.*
> 3 We use a period at the end of a sentence.
>   *... a lot of people from other countries live and work there.*

5 ACTIVATE Follow the steps in the writing guide.

Country and language report: Canada

1 Canada is a large country in North America. It has a border with the United States in the south. The Atlantic Ocean is to the east of Canada and the Pacific Ocean is to the west. The capital of Canada is Ottawa and the currency is the Canadian dollar.

2 The official languages of Canada are English and French. Most Canadians speak English, but French is the main language in the Quebec area. All students study English and French in schools, but people also study Spanish, German, and Mandarin.

3 The population of Canada is about 34 million and a lot of people from other countries live and work there. In big cities, like Vancouver and Toronto, over thirty percent of the population comes from outside Canada. In particular, there are a lot of people from Europe, Asia, and the U.S., but there are also people from Africa and South America.

○ WRITING GUIDE

A TASK

Write a *Country and language report* about your country.

B THINK AND PLAN

1 Where is your country?
2 What other countries does it have borders with?
3 What is the capital city and the currency?
4 What are the official languages and where do people speak them?
5 What languages do people study at school?
6 What is the population of your country?
7 Do many people of other nationalities live in your country? Where are they from?

C WRITE

Paragraph 1: The country
... is a (large) country in ...
Paragraph 2: Languages
The official language(s) of ...
Paragraph 3: People from other countries
The population of ...

D CHECK

• punctuation   • key phrases   • paragraphs

Vocabulary

1 Complete the sentences with the correct form of the words in the box.

> country language nationality person
> city class population

1 There are about 500 million ___ in the European Union.
2 Seattle and Los Angeles are ___ in the west of the U.S.
3 There are 27 ___ in the European Union.
4 There are people of 179 different ___ living in New York.
5 In Canada, there are two official ___.
6 There are ___ in French and Spanish in my school.
7 The ___ of New York is more than 8.2 million.

2 Match the verbs in the box with words 1–8.

> watch ~~have~~ do go start work
> speak cook

1 **have** lunch
2 ___ Spanish
3 ___ TV
4 ___ to bed
5 ___ in a factory
6 ___ dinner
7 ___ school
8 ___ my homework

Language focus

3 Complete the sentences with the affirmative or negative forms of the verbs in exercise 2.

1 Colette ___ DVDs after dinner. ✘
2 I ___ to bed at about eleven o'clock every night. ✔
3 We ___ lunch at school. ✘
4 Billy ___ his homework before dinner. ✔
5 My parents ___ Spanish fluently. ✔
6 My brother ___ in an office. ✘
7 Jim and I ___ school at nine o'clock. ✔
8 Dad ___ dinner on the weekend. ✘

4 Write questions and answers about the sentences in exercise 3.

> *Does Colette watch DVDs after dinner?*
>
> *No, she doesn't.*

5 Write questions for these answers with the words in parentheses.

I have Spanish classes <u>twice a week</u>. (How often)
How often do you have Spanish classes?
1 Tania lives in <u>New York</u>. (Where)
2 Tom and Jim have lunch at <u>12:30</u>. (What time)
3 I usually get up at <u>7 a.m.</u> (When)
4 I sit next to <u>Sarah</u> in class. (Who)
5 I read <u>comic books</u>. (What)
6 I practice the trumpet <u>three times a week</u>. (How often)

Communication

6 Complete the mini-dialogues with the words in the box.

> do enjoy mind doing

Boy What do you like [1]___ after school?
Girl I really [2]___ playing video games.
Boy [3]___ you like reading?
Girl I don't [4]___ reading comic books, but I hate books.

> singing enjoy loves about

Girl Do you [5]___ playing in the group?
Boy Yes, I do. I don't like [6]___.
Girl What [7]___ Julia?
Boy Oh, she [8]___ dancing.

Listening

7 🔊 1.40 Listen and complete the text.

There are 600 [1]___ in Marc's school and they are from about [2]___ different countries. There are classes in French, Spanish, and [3]___ at the school. Marc's parents come from [4]___ and they often go to Quebec for the weekend. Marc and his sister study [5]___ because they speak French fluently. Marc [6]___ meets his friends after school and they often play [7]___ in the park. In the evening, he always [8]___ soccer on TV.

PROJECT ⬤ City profile

1 What do you know about Sydney? Cover the text and answer the questions.

1 Which country is it in?
2 Which part of the country is it in?
3 Is it the capital city?
4 How many people live there?
5 What is the main language?
6 Do you know any tourist sights in Sydney?

2 Now read the text and check your answers.

SYDNEY

Sydney is the largest city in Australia with a population of 4.6 million. It is on the east coast of Australia, on the Pacific Ocean. Sydney is not the capital of Australia. The capital city is Canberra, a small city 280 kilometers southwest of Sydney.

Most people speak English, but you can hear many other languages in Sydney. Thirty percent of the population is from other countries and there are always a lot of tourists.

Popular tourist sights include the famous Sydney Harbour Bridge. Tourists like to walk along the bridge to get an amazing view of the city. Some even do the bridge climb, a fantastic walk to the top, 134 meters above the harbor!

The Sydney Opera House is one of the most famous buildings in the world. It looks like a group of giant seashells and houses a lot of concert halls and theaters.

There are 70 beaches in Sydney. Bondi Beach is the most famous of them. People come here from all over the world to surf the big waves. Tourists love to spend Christmas Day here and eat Christmas dinner on the beach!

3 Make a poster about a famous city. Follow the steps in the project checklist.

> ## ⬤ PROJECT CHECKLIST
>
> **1** Work in small groups. Choose a famous city to write about.
> **2** Find information on the Internet about:
>
> - where the city is
> - what the population is
> - what the main language is
> - some popular tourist sights
>
> If you can, add more information.
>
> **3** Write a short text about the city using the information you found.
> **4** Find some pictures of the popular tourist sights.
> **5** Find a map of the country to show the location of the city.
> **6** Make a poster with your text, map, and pictures.
> **7** Present your city to the rest of the class.

The wild side

Start thinking

1 What do polar bears eat?
2 Do sharks usually attack humans?
3 What type of animal is on the "red list"?

Aims

Communication: I can ...

- describe animals.
- understand an article about animals in danger.
- talk about things happening now.
- understand an interview about animal behavior.
- ask people about their routines and what they are doing now.
- talk about what I'm doing now.
- write an article about an animal.

Vocabulary

- Animals
- Verbs: animal behavior

Language focus

- Present continuous: affirmative and negative
- Present continuous: questions
- Present continuous and simple present
- *because*

Reach Out Options

Extra listening and speaking
Talking about future arrangements
⇨ Page 91

Curriculum extra
Natural science: Animals
⇨ Page 99

Culture
National parks
⇨ Page 107

Vocabulary puzzles
Animals; Animal behavior
⇨ Page 115

VOCABULARY ■ Animals
I can describe animals.

1 Match the animals in the box with pictures 1–16 in the *Eye to Eye* quiz on page 39. Which picture is not an eye?

> snake   frog   elephant   bear   parrot   owl   human   shark   crocodile   whale   spider   seal   butterfly   falcon   chameleon   fly

2 Look at the key phrases. Which phrases do we use for things we see and which for things we hear? Which can be used for both?

> **KEY PHRASES ◯ Speculating about things you see and hear**
>
> It looks like a / an ….   It doesn't look like a / an ….
> It sounds like a / an ….   It doesn't sound like a / an ….
> Maybe it's a / an ….   I'm sure it's a / an ….

3 🔊 2.02 Compare your answers to exercise 1 using the key phrases. Then listen and check.

4 🔊 2.03 Listen and identify the animals. Use the key phrases in exercise 2.

> It sounds like a …
> Yes, maybe it's a …

5 Check the meaning of the words in blue. Then choose an animal in exercise 1 and answer questions 1–8.

1 Does it live in this country?
2 Does it attack humans?
3 Does it eat meat?
4 Does it swim?
5 Does it fly?
6 Does it have more than four legs?
7 Does it climb trees?
8 Does it hunt fish?

6 **ACTIVATE** Work in pairs. Each think of an animal. Then ask questions to guess your partner's animal. Use the questions in exercise 5 and your own ideas.

> Does it swim?
> No, it doesn't.
> Does it hunt small animals?
> Yes, it does.

> ◯ *Finished?*
> **Look at the animals in exercise 1. Which animals are: birds, insects, mammals, fish, reptiles? Make a mind map. Which two animals don't go in any of the categories?**

Eye to Eye

How many animals can you identify?
Which picture is not an eye?

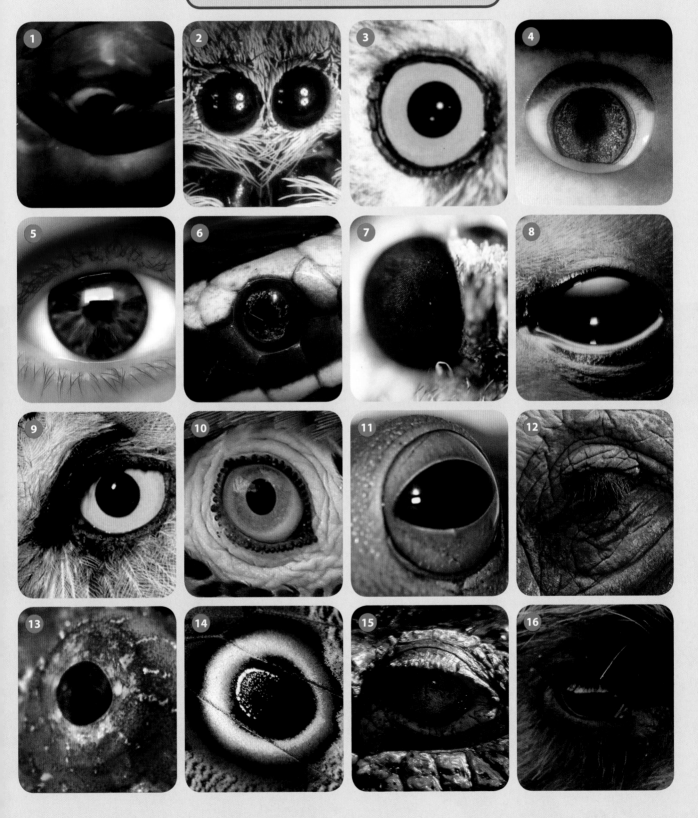

1 ● 2.04 Read the title of the article and the question. What do you think the answer is? Why? Read and listen to the text and check your answer.

2 Read the text again. Choose the correct answers.

1 Crocodiles are more dangerous than ___
   a sharks. **b** chairs. **c** people.
2 Sharks attack ___ people every year.
   a 100 **b** 7 or 8 **c** 3 or 4
3 People kill animals ___
   a just for food.
   b mainly for fur or fun.
   c for meat, fun, and fur.
4 The "red list" is a list of ___
   a red animals.
   b dangerous animals.
   c animals becoming extinct.
5 The writer wants readers to ___
   a change their actions.
   b save tigers and elephants.
   c stop eating meat.

3 BUILD YOUR VOCABULARY Look at the words in blue in the text. Which two words are verbs? Use the words to complete the sentences.

1 Sharks don't often ___ humans.
2 There are ___ 6,000 wild tigers in the world.
3 Some people are trying to ___ the tigers.
4 There are more ___ with cars than with animals.
5 Human ___ are changing the climate.
6 There is a lot of ___ in big cities.

4 ABOUT YOU Answer the questions. Then compare your answers with a partner.

1 Which animals do you like / dislike? Why?
2 Which animals are endangered in your country? Why?
3 What are people doing to save these animals?
4 Do people hunt animals in your country? Why?
5 Is pollution a problem where you live? Why?

Danger! Humans!

? Which is more dangerous: a shark, a chair, or a person?

When an animal attacks a person, there are always stories about it on TV and in the newspapers. But people are usually more dangerous than animals. Every year, we kill approximately 100 million sharks, but sharks only attack three or four people, and crocodiles six or seven. More people die in accidents with chairs!

Animals aren't really a problem for people, but we are a problem for animals. We eat millions of tons of fish and meat every year. But people don't kill animals just for food. They also hunt them for fur or for fun. While you're reading this, people are hunting whales in the Arctic, tigers in Asia, and elephants in Africa.

Right now, animals are becoming extinct in every part of the world. The "red list" of animals in danger includes insects, frogs, chameleons, fish, and bigger animals, like bears and whales. We aren't killing all these animals directly, but they are dying and becoming extinct because of human actions. Our pollution and construction is changing the climate and animals' habitats, and time is running out for some animals. It's important to change our actions now and save the animals!

1 Complete the sentences from the text on page 40. Then choose the correct words in rules a–c.

Animals ¹___ becoming extinct.

We ²___ killing all these animals directly.

Our pollution ³___ changing the climate.

⭕ RULES

a We use the present continuous to talk about **things happening now / habits and routines**.

b We use the verb *do / be* to form the present continuous.

c We add *-ing / -ed* to the main verb in the present continuous.

2 Find the present continuous form of verbs 1–6 in the text on page 40. Then read the spelling rules and match the verbs to spelling rules 1–3. Which verb doesn't match any rule?

1 become	**3** hunt	**5** run
2 die	**4** change	**6** read

⭕ SPELLING RULES

1 Most verbs → + *-ing*:
meet – meeting;   play – playing

2 Verbs ending in *-e* → remove *-e* + *-ing*:
have – having;   write – writing

3 Verbs ending in a vowel + consonant → double final consonant + *-ing*:
swim – swimming;   stop – stopping

(More practice ⇨ Workbook page 33)

3 🔊 2.05 Listen to the sounds. Match the things in A with the actions in B. Then write sentences describing the actions using the present continuous.

I *Two dogs are running in the park.*

A	B
1 Two dogs	(attack) a mosquito.
2 A parrot	(make) a cake.
3 A man	(practice) the piano.
4 A whale	(speak) English.
5 Children	(sing) to its partner.
6 A girl	(have) a meal.
7 A lion	(run) in the park.

(Pronunciation: *-ing* ⇨ Workbook page 91)

4 Work in pairs. Read the prompts and look at the picture. Make affirmative and negative sentences using the present continuous.

child / sit / by the river (stand)

> *A child isn't sitting by the river.*
> *She is standing by the river.*

1 child / feed / bears (ducks)

2 falcon / sleep (hunt)

3 two people / watch / chameleon (falcon)

4 three people / swim (run)

5 Write sentences about what is happening now.

I / think about the weekend

I'm not thinking about the weekend.

1 my parents / work

2 the teacher / write on the board

3 I / sit next to a girl

4 we / work hard

5 I / wear jeans

6 the student by the door / listen

6 **ACTIVATE** Think of a person in your class and write one affirmative and one negative sentence using the present continuous. Swap your sentences with your partner and guess his or her person.

He's wearing a green T-shirt. He isn't listening to the teacher.

(Is it Tom?)   (Yes, it is.)

⭕ *Finished?*

Imagine a perfect day in a perfect place with your family or friends. Write sentences describing where you are and what is happening.

I'm walking in the mountains with my friends. We're …

1 Check the meaning of the verbs in bold. Then look at pictures 1–6 and choose the correct verbs.

1 The blackbird is **feeding** / **eating** its chicks.
2 The beaver is **digging** / **building** a dam.
3 The chameleon is **catching** / **helping** an insect with its tongue.
4 The fish is **fighting** / **protecting** the other fish.
5 The bear is **hunting** / **hiding** the salmon.
6 A falcon is **playing with** / **chasing** a group of smaller birds.

2 Complete the sentences with names of animals. Compare your answers with a partner.

Owls hunt at night. They eat small animals.

1 ___ hide in trees. They don't have legs.
2 ___ catch fish. They sleep in the winter.
3 ___ don't feed their young. They can change color when they want to hide.
4 ___ hunt smaller fish. They sometimes attack humans.
5 ___ build houses. They catch animals and put them in zoos.
6 ___ protect their babies from sharks. They sing to each other.

3 ● 2.06 Listen to an interview with Mike. Which of the pictures does Mike speak about?

4 ● 2.06 Try to complete the text. Then listen again and check your answers.

Blackbirds feed their chicks every day for ¹___ weeks. In the second picture, the chameleon is catching a ²___. The chameleon sometimes catches insects from a distance of ³___ centimeters! The big fish is a goliath grouper and it is ⁴___ meters long. It isn't attacking the small ⁵___, it is protecting them. In the last picture, a falcon is hunting small birds. It's a very fast bird and it sometimes ⁶___ at 390 kilometers an hour.

5 Choose an animal you know and answer the questions.

1 How big is the animal? (enormous, not very big, not very small, tiny)
2 Where does it live? (in trees, the ocean, rivers, your house, holes, other)
3 What does it eat? (meat, other animals, grass, fruit, other)
4 How does it move? (swim, walk, run, fly)

6 ACTIVATE Interview your partner about his or her animal. Use your answers in exercise 5.

How big is your animal? | It isn't very big.

LANGUAGE FOCUS ■ Present continuous: questions • Present continuous and simple present

I can ask people about their routines and what they are doing now.

4

Present continuous: questions

1 Complete the questions from the listening on page 42. Can you remember the answers?

1 What ___ the chameleon catching?
2 ___ the big fish hunting the smaller fish?
3 ___ the bigger bird attacking the others?

2 Match the questions in exercise 1 with answers a–c. Then complete the rules.

a No, it isn't.
b Yes, it is.
c A fly.

◯ RULES

1 We make affirmative short answers with *Yes,* + pronoun + *am /* ^{1}___ */ are.*
2 We make negative short answers with *No,* + pronoun + *'m not / isn't /* ^{2}___.

(More practice ⇨ Workbook page 35)

3 Write questions for the answers using the words in parentheses.

Ron **What are you watching?** (what / you / watch)
Emi I'm watching those seals. Look!
Ron ^{1}___? (where / those seals / swim to)
Emi They're swimming to the beach.
Ron ^{2}___? (why / do / that)
Emi Because there are sharks near.
Ron ^{3}___? (what / that seal / do)
Emi She's protecting her baby.
Ron ^{4}___? (who / watch / the seals / in that small boat)
Emi They're scientists.
Ron ^{5}___? (why / watch / the seals)
Emi Because they're counting them.
Ron ^{6}___? (where / that scientist / go)
Emi I don't know. Be quiet!

4 Ask and answer questions about the information in exercise 3.

Where / Ron and Emi / stand

(**Where are Ron and Emi standing?**) (On a boat.)

1 what / Emi / watch
2 the seals / sit / on the rocks
3 why / the seals / swim / to the beach
4 the seal / attack / the shark
5 who / count / the seals
6 the scientist / go

Present continuous and simple present

5 Complete the table with sentences 1–6. Which time expressions in bold do we use with: (a) the simple present, (b) the present continuous?

1 She studies **every day**.
2 She's studying **today**.
3 I **always** walk to school.
4 I'm walking **right now**.
5 We don't **usually** eat meat.
6 We aren't eating meat **now**.

Simple present Routine or repeated action	Present continuous Action happening now
She studies every day.	She's studying today.

(More practice ⇨ Workbook page 35)

6 Complete the sentences. Use the simple present and present continuous forms of the verbs.

He usually **goes to school** (go to school) by car, but today he**'s walking** (walk).

1 I ___ (listen) to rap music right now.
  I ___ (prefer) heavy metal.
2 They ___ (not usually go) to the movie theater. They ___ (watch) a DVD right now.
3 They ___ (go) to bed late every day. They ___ (sleep) now.
4 He ___ (always play) soccer after school, but he ___ (play) tennis today.
5 She ___ (have) dinner now. She ___ (like) fish.

7 **ACTIVATE** Write six questions to ask your partner about now and at home. Use the simple present and present continuous forms of the verbs in the box. Then ask and answer questions with your partner.

listen to   study   read   ~~wear~~
talk about   practice   write   watch

(**What do you wear at home?**) (I wear ...)

(**What are you wearing now?**) (I'm wearing ...)

◯ *Finished?*
Write sentences with the time expressions in exercise 5. Use the simple present and the present continuous.
I play the guitar every day. I'm thinking about ...

Tina	Hello.
Jake	Hey, Tina. It's Jake.
Tina	Hi there. How are you?
Jake	Fine, thanks. What are you doing right now?
Tina	I'm sightseeing! I'm at the Miami aquarium with Laura. It's called the Miami Seaquarium.
Jake	Really? What are you looking at?
Tina	Oh, there are some sharks here. They're really cool.
Jake	Are you having a good time?
Tina	Yeah, it's really interesting. We can meet later if you want.
Jake	OK, great! Give me a call.
Tina	Sure. Bye for now.

1 Look at the picture. Where is Tina?

2 ⏺ 2.07 Listen to the dialogue and check your answer in exercise 1. What is Tina doing?

3 ⏺ 2.07 Match the key phrases with the responses in blue in the dialogue. Then listen again and practice the dialogue.

KEY PHRASES ◯ Talking on the phone

1 Are you having a good time?
2 Give me a call.
3 It's (Jake).
4 We can meet later if you want.
5 What are you doing right now?
6 How are you?

STUDY STRATEGY ◯ Improving pronunciation

4 ⏺ 2.08 Listen and repeat. Practice linking the words.

1 How‿are you?
2 What‿are you doing?
3 There‿are some sharks here.
4 Are you having‿a good time?
5 It's really‿interesting.

5 ⏺ 2.09 Complete the mini-dialogue with the key phrases. Listen and check. Then practice the mini-dialogue.

Sal	Hello.
Ben	Hi, Sal. ¹___ Ben.
Sal	Hi, there! ²___ right now?
Ben	I'm at the skateboard park with Tom. We're practicing.
Sal	Really? ³___ a good time?
Ben	Yeah. It's fun. We can meet later ⁴___.
Sal	OK. ⁵___ a call.
Ben	Sure. Bye for now.

6 ACTIVATE Work in pairs. Prepare a new dialogue using the dialogue in exercise 5 as a model. Change the words in blue. Use ideas from the box or your own ideas. Practice the new dialogue.

> shopping mall / shopping
> library / studying
> park / playing soccer
> community center / playing tennis
> lake / swimming

WRITING ■ A description of a wildlife picture
I can write an article about an animal.

4

"Red list" animals: The orca

1 The animals in this picture are orcas or "killer whales". In fact, an orca is not a whale, but a type of dolphin. Here they are swimming in a group near the shore. Maybe they're hunting for seals.

2 Orcas live in all of the world's oceans. They hunt and play in groups. They are aggressive and they usually eat fish, squid, seals, and turtles. Females have one baby, called a calf, every two or three years.

3 Orcas are on the "red list" because they are in danger of becoming extinct. Some orcas are in danger because there is pollution in the ocean. They also die in fishing nets. I think that it is important to protect these animals.

1 **Read the model text and answer the questions.**

1 Which paragraph describes the life and habitat of the orca? Which describes a problem?
2 Do orcas live in groups?
3 What do orcas eat?
4 How often do females have calves?
5 Why are they becoming extinct?

Language point: *because*

2 **Match sentences 1–6 with a–f. Combine the sentences using *because*.**

1 Orcas are in danger.
2 They're hunting.
3 I don't swim.
4 She's having a good time.
5 He's running.
6 They're hiding.

a I don't like the water.
b He's late.
c There is pollution in the ocean.
d They're scared.
e They're hungry.
f She's at the aquarium.

3 Match the key phrases a–e with paragraphs 1–3 in exercise 1.

> **KEY PHRASES ◯ Describing wildlife**
>
> a Females have (one baby), called a (calf), every … .
> b (Orcas) live in … .
> c Here they are … .
> d (Orcas) are on the "red list" because … .
> e The animals in this picture are … .

4 **ACTIVATE** Follow the steps in the writing guide.

> **◯ WRITING GUIDE**
>
> **A TASK**
>
> Look at the picture below and write an article about polar bears.
>
> **B THINK AND PLAN**
>
> Read the notes below about polar bears and match a–e in exercise 3 with paragraph titles 1–3.
>
> **Paragraph 1:** Introduction: *e*
> **Paragraph 2:** Life and habitat:
> **Paragraph 3:** Problems:
>
> **C WRITE**
>
> Write your article and follow your paragraph plan. Use the model text and the key phrases.
>
> **D CHECK**
>
> • the use of *because*

Notes: The polar bear

a females: two babies / cubs / every four or five years
b "red list":
climate / change ➔ ice / melt; pollution; hunting ➔ fur
c habitat: the Arctic / on ice
d food: seals and fish
e this picture:
polar bears / on ice; hunt / seals
f picture: a female with two cubs
g behavior: aggressive; hunt seals; can swim

Vocabulary

1 Choose the correct words.

1 Humans **kill** / **die** seals for their fur.
2 Crocodiles **feed** / **eat** meat.
3 Falcons **build** / **hide** in trees.
4 Rabbits **climb** / **dig** holes in the ground.
5 Female elephants **attack** / **protect** their babies.
6 Bears **catch** / **fight** fish in rivers.
7 Whales don't **fly** / **swim**.
8 Some snakes can **climb** / **chase** trees.

2 Complete the text with the words in the box.

> habitat   live   swim   climate   extinct
> pollution   hunt

Polar bears are becoming ¹___. Why? Human ²___ is changing the ³___. Polar bears ⁴___ on the ice in the Arctic. But the ice is melting and their ⁵___ is getting smaller. Every year it gets more difficult for the bears to ⁶___ seals. Polar bears can ⁷___, but they can't live in the ocean!

Language focus

3 Write sentences using the correct form of the present continuous.

1 he / catch fish for dinner
2 we / study the climate
3 those crocodiles / not sleep
4 I / watch a TV program about polar bears
5 they / not do their homework
6 she / write a book about whales
7 you / not listen to me

4 Write questions and short answers. Use the present continuous.

you / write an e-mail ✔
Are you writing an e-mail? Yes, I am.

1 the climate / change ✔
2 tigers / become extinct ✔
3 you / talk to Billy ✘
4 that female bear / protect her baby ✔
5 we / learn new vocabulary ✔
6 your friends / run in the park now ✘
7 Jack / look for his book ✘

5 Complete the sentences with the present continuous or the simple present.

1 a We ___ (watch) TV every day.
    b We ___ (watch) a good documentary now.
2 a I ___ (swim) in the ocean every year.
    b Oh no! That shark ___ (swim) towards us.
3 a He ___ (eat) in a restaurant right now.
    b He usually ___ (eat) at home.
4 a Humans sometimes ___ (hunt) animals for sport.
    b Look! Those men ___ (hunt) baby seals.

Communication

6 Complete the dialogue with the phrases in the box.

> It sounds like   I'm reading   every day
> It looks like   a good time   Maybe it's
> What are you doing

Paul   ¹___ right now?
Anna   ²___ an e-mail from Emma. She's in Australia.
Paul   Is she having ³___?
Anna   Yes, she says it's fantastic. She goes swimming ⁴___.
Paul   Listen! What's that?
Anna   ⁵___ a mosquito.
Paul   Well, it isn't a mosquito.
Anna   Look. It's yellow and black. ⁶___ a wasp.
Paul   I'm not sure it is.
Anna   ⁷___ a bee.
Paul   That's OK, then.

Listening

7 ● 2.10 Listen to a conversation and choose the correct words.

1 Harry is with **Lily** / **Mark**.
2 They are at **the park** / **a café**.
3 There's a **movie** / **music** festival there.
4 He's having a **terrible** / **fantastic** time.
5 The weather is very **cold** / **hot**.
6 Lily can call Harry at **four** / **five** o'clock.

4

Listening

1 Look at the animals in the pictures. What are they? Where can you see these animals?

2 🔘 2.11 Listen to a conversation. Which two pictures are Jon's?

3 🔘 2.11 Listen again and complete the sentences.

1 Jon enjoys taking ___.
2 The dolphins are ___ in front of the boat.
3 Jon and his dad often see ___ and ___.
4 Sea crocodiles are ___ than sharks.
5 Sea crocodiles live in Australia, ___, and ___.
6 Sea crocodiles are becoming ___ in many countries.
7 Where Pierre comes from, people speak ___.
8 Tim is buying a ___ at the shopping mall.

Speaking

4 Work in pairs and prepare a conversation. You are describing this picture to your partner. Imagine that the two people in the picture are from different countries. Answer the questions.

- Where is the place in the picture?
- Who are the people in the picture?
- What nationality are they?
- What country do they come from?
- What are the people doing in the picture?
- What is the animal?
- What is it doing?

5 Have a conversation. Use your ideas in exercise 4 and the chart below to help you. One of you is A, one of you is B. Change roles.

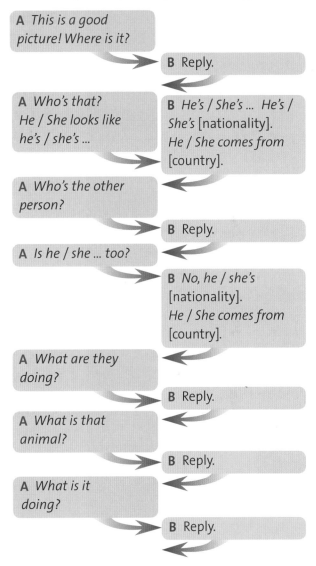

A *This is a good picture! Where is it?*

B *Reply.*

A *Who's that? He / She looks like he's / she's …*

B *He's / She's … He's / She's [nationality]. He / She comes from [country].*

A *Who's the other person?*

B *Reply.*

A *Is he / she … too?*

B *No, he / she's [nationality]. He / She comes from [country].*

A *What are they doing?*

B *Reply.*

A *What is that animal?*

B *Reply.*

A *What is it doing?*

B *Reply.*

Writing

6 Write an e-mail to a friend. You are on vacation and you are sending a wildlife picture to your friend. Talk about your vacation and describe the picture in exercise 4 or another picture. Use the questions in exercise 4 to help you. Begin like this:

Hi … ,
I'm having a fantastic vacation here in … .
I'm staying … . Here is a picture of … .
Here they are … .

In and out of school

Start thinking

1 Are there any boarding schools in your country?
2 Which activities can you do after school?
3 Does your school have a cafeteria?

Aims

Communication: I can ...

- talk about my school schedule and after-school activities.
- understand an interview about boarding school life.
- talk about things we can and can't do.
- talk about my eating habits.
- talk about food and meals.
- make, accept, and refuse invitations.
- write an e-mail about my school.

Vocabulary

- Activities in and out of school
- Food and drink

Language focus

- *can* for ability and permission
- Countable and uncountable nouns: *a / an, the, some, any, much, many,* and *a lot of*
- Giving examples

Reach Out Options

Extra listening and speaking

Ordering food

⇨ Page 92

Curriculum extra

Physical education:
Rules of a game

⇨ Page 100

Culture

Home schooling

⇨ Page 108

Vocabulary puzzles

Activities in and out of school; Food and drink

⇨ Page 116

VOCABULARY ■ Activities in and out of school

I can talk about my school schedule and after-school activities.

1 🔊 2.17 Match eight of the words in the box with pictures 1–8 on page 49. Then listen and check.

1 P.E.

> math   science   basketball   music   history
> chess   soccer   dance   geography   drama
> P.E.*   computer science   French   art

*Physical Education

2 Do the *Test your knowledge* quiz on page 49. Who has the most answers right?

3 Check the meaning of phrases 1–5. Match other words in exercise 1 with the words in blue.

1 dance practice
2 history test
3 math homework
4 computer science class
5 soccer game

4 🔊 2.18 Listen to Luke and Emily talk about activities. Complete the sentences. What is their favorite day?

1 Today's a good day for Emily because she has ___ this afternoon.
2 Mr. Parnell gives Luke's class a history ___ every Monday.
3 Tuesday isn't a good day for Luke because he has two ___ classes in the morning.
4 On Wednesday afternoons, Luke has ___ at two o'clock.
5 Luke has basketball ___ after school three times a week.
6 Luke has a basketball ___ once a month.
7 Mr. Parnell gives all his ___ a test once a week.

5 Study the key phrases. Find similar phrases in the sentences in exercise 4. Which words are different in these phrases?

> **KEY PHRASES ◯ Time expressions**
>
> once a day   today   every Tuesday
> twice a month   this morning   on Friday morning(s)
> three times a week   at five o'clock   in the afternoon

6 **ACTIVATE** Write sentences about your routines and activities using the key phrases. Then interview your partner. What's his / her favorite day?

I have swimming practice once a week.
We have an English test on Friday.

> How often do you have baseball practice?

> I have baseball practice three times a week.

> When do we have a math test?

> We have a math test on Monday afternoon.

2 Which disk has more space?

a a 1 megabyte disk
b a 1 gigabyte disk
c a 1 terabyte disk

3 Four people can make eight chairs in two days. How many chairs can two people make in one day?

a two　　b four　　c six

1 Which sport is most popular in American schools?

a soccer
b basketball
c baseball

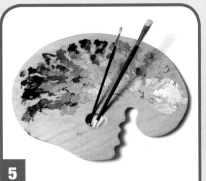

5 What two colors make purple?

a red and orange
b blue and red
c blue and green

6 How many of these elements are gases: Oxygen (O), Neon (Ne), Magnesium (Mg), Aluminum (Al)?

a one　　b two　　c four

4 How many black and white pieces are there in this game?

a sixteen
b twenty-four
c thirty-two

7 You're traveling by train from Spain to The Netherlands. Which of these countries is on your route?

a France
b France and Italy
c France and Belgium

8 These students are in a drama class. What are they studying?

a a painting by Picasso
b a play by Shakespeare
c a book by Darwin

O Finished?
Write sentences about your week. Which days are good? Which days are bad? Why?
I don't like Mondays because I have two hours of science.

1 What do you know about boarding schools? How are they different to other schools?

2 🔵 2.19 Read about Michael's day. Match questions a–h with paragraphs 1–7. There is one extra question. Then listen and check.

a What activities do you do?
b What do you like about boarding school?
c Can you describe your typical day?
d What do you do on your vacations?
e Do you have any free time?
f Are you ever homesick?
g What do you do on the weekend?
h Is the food OK?

3 Read the text again and answer the questions.

1 What time do classes start in the morning?
2 How often does Michael have orchestra practice?
3 When can students watch TV?
4 Where can students go on Sundays?
5 Who does Michael share a bedroom with?
6 How often does Michael see his parents?

4 BUILD YOUR VOCABULARY Find verbs in the text that go with the words in 1–6.

1 **be** homesick
2 ___ a room
3 ___ a break
4 ___ with friends
5 ___ busy
6 ___ abroad

5 ABOUT YOU Ask and answer the questions.

1 What do you think is good or bad about boarding school?
2 What do you like about your school?
3 What extra activities can you do?
4 What do you do at break time at school?
5 What differences are there between Michael's school day and your day?

Living at school

1 ___
Yes. We get up at 6:45 and have breakfast at 7:15. Classes are from 8:00 until 3:30, with an hour for lunch at 12:50. After classes we have activities from 4:15 to 6:00, and then dinner is at 6:15. We do our homework at 7:30 and bedtime is at 10:30.

2 ___
I play soccer twice a week. I can play the violin and I'm in the school orchestra. We practice three times a week.

3 ___
We don't have much free time during the week. We take a break before homework when we can relax, chat with friends, or watch TV. We have Sundays free.

4 ___
There are classes on Saturday mornings, then sports and free-time activities in the afternoon. Sometimes we can go to the swimming pool on Sundays.

5 ___
It isn't bad. You can choose your food. There's a cafeteria with salads, pizzas, sandwiches, and different "specials" every day.

6 ___
I like sharing a room with my best friend. Also, we have everything here at school – tennis courts, a gym, computers, and sports fields. That's great.

7 ___
Sometimes, but people here are friendly and we're really busy. I can't live at home because my parents work abroad. I see them three times a year on my vacation.

LANGUAGE FOCUS ■ *can* for ability and permission

I can talk about things we can and can't do.

1 Look at the sentences and answer the questions.

  a You can go to the swimming pool.
  b I can play the piano. Listen!
  c Arrgh! Tom can't sing!
  d We can't go into town.
  e Can they speak Spanish?

  1 Which two sentences are about permission?
  2 Which three sentences are about ability?
  3 What is the negative form of *can*?
  4 Do we use *do* and *does* to make questions with *can*?

2 Look at the sentences and write P (permission) or A (ability).

  1 I can swim. ☑
  2 You can't use your cell phone in class. ☐
  3 My father can speak German and Portuguese. ☐
  4 You can wear jeans if you want. ☐
  5 You can go to the movies this evening. ☐
  6 Yuck! You can't cook. ☐

(More practice ⇨ Workbook page 41)

3 Write sentences about your abilities. Use the ideas in the box. Then ask and answer with a partner.

I can't play chess.

> play chess   speak three languages
> run one kilometer   play an instrument
> swim twenty-five meters
> name six countries in English
> dance the tango   stand on my head

(Can you play chess?)   (No, I can't.)

4 Write about things you can or can't do at your school. Use the phrases below and your own ideas.

> use cell phones   talk during a test
> wear jeans   go home for lunch
> eat at school   listen to music

We can't use cell phones in class.

5 🔊 2.20 Look at the key phrases. Complete the dialogue. Then listen and check.

> **KEY PHRASES ○ Requesting, giving, and refusing permission**
>
> Is it OK if I ... ?   No, sorry, you can't.
> Why not?   Yes, you can.
> Can I / we ... ?

Nathan Mom, **is it OK if** I go to Shaun's house?
Mom No, sorry, ¹you can't
Nathan I can't? ²Why not
Mom Because your grandparents are here this afternoon.
Nathan Oh, right. ³Can I if I go this evening, then?
Mom No, not this evening, Nathan. You have a lot of homework.
Nathan Well, ⁴can I go tomorrow?
Mom Yes, ⁵you can
Nathan Great. Thanks.

6 **ACTIVATE** Work in pairs. Practice the dialogue in exercise 5. Then change the words in blue and practice a new dialogue.

> ○ *Finished?*
> **Write about things you can and can't do at home.**
> *I can watch TV until 10:30 p.m.*
> *I can't stay out late on school nights.*

School lunch

What are modern American children eating? At lunchtime, Becky Jackson goes to a fast food restaurant and buys a hamburger, some French fries, some ice cream, and a soda. Some of her friends buy food at fast food restaurants, too. School meals are healthier, but Becky and her friends don't like them and they never eat in the school cafeteria.

Who's having a healthy lunch at school? *The Monday Documentary* reports from three other countries ...

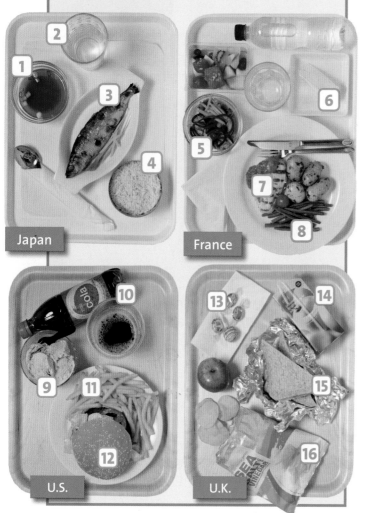

Japan

France

U.S.

U.K.

1 🔘 2.21 **Match 1–16 in the photos with words in the box. Then listen and check.**

> salad   French fries   soup   candy   fish
> apple   bread   rice   pasta   nuts   egg
> potato chips   sandwich   beans   water
> hamburger   cheese   soda   juice
> ice cream   meat

Pronunciation: /ɪ/ and /i/ ⟹ Workbook page 91

2 **Think of two more words to add to each group.**

1 meat: chicken, ___, ___
2 vegetables: potato, ___, ___
3 fruit: pear, ___, ___
4 drinks: juice, ___, ___

3 **Ask and answer the questions with a partner. Then read the key.**

Healthy eating

Do you eat more ...
1 French fries or vegetables?
2 ice cream or cheese?
3 soda or juice?
4 candy or salad?
5 potato chips or nuts?
6 meat or fish?
7 hamburgers or rice?

Key — **Green** answers mean your diet is probably OK. **Orange** answers mean you can probably improve your diet.

4 🔘 2.22 **Look at the school lunches in the pictures and read the text. Which lunch is very healthy and which is very unhealthy? Listen and check.**

5 🔘 2.22 **Listen to the program again and choose the correct answers.**

1 There **aren't any / are a lot of** vegetables on the menu in the U.S. today.
2 **A lot of / Some** American teenagers eat school lunches.
3 **There aren't many / There are a lot of** vending machines in American schools.
4 Japanese students **eat / don't eat** soup for lunch.
5 There **isn't much / is a lot of** junk food in French schools.

6 ACTIVATE **Ask and answer the questions.**

1 What do you eat for lunch at school?
2 Which lunch in the pictures do you like / not like?
3 What healthy / unhealthy food do you eat?
4 What fruit and vegetables do you like / not like?
5 What's your favorite meal?

LANGUAGE FOCUS ■ Countable and uncountable nouns:
a / an, the, some, any, much, many, and *a lot of*
I can talk about food and meals.

5

1 Study the rules. Match the words in blue in the text below with rules 1–4.

> **◯ RULES**
>
> **1** We use *a/an* to talk about something for the first time.
> **2** We use *a/an* with singular countable nouns.
> **3** We use *the* when there is only one.
> **4** We use *the* to talk about something again.

At lunchtime, Becky Jackson buys a hamburger and some ice cream. She goes to a fast food restaurant near her school. Her friend Annie goes to the fast food restaurant, too. But Becky's other friends have lunch at the school cafeteria.

(More practice ⇨ Workbook page 43)

2 Complete the text with *a / an* and *the.*

There's ¹___ good restaurant near my school. I often go to ²___ restaurant and I buy ³___ hamburger and ⁴___ soda for lunch. There's ⁵___ vending machine near my classroom. I sometimes buy ⁶___ candy bar from ⁷___ machine. I never eat at ⁸___ school cafeteria because I don't like the food.

3 Look at the pictures and complete the table with the words in the box.

> water   potato chips   pasta   rice
> vegetables   cheese   pears

Uncountable	Countable
There's a lot of **pasta**.	There are a lot of ⁴___.
There's some ¹___.	There are some ⁵___.
There isn't much ²___.	There aren't many grapes.
There isn't any ³___.	There aren't any ⁶___.

(More practice ⇨ Workbook page 43)

4 Look at the sentences in exercise 3 and choose the correct words in the rules.

> **◯ RULES**
>
> **1** We always use a **singular / plural** verb with uncountable nouns.
> **2** We use *much / many* with uncountable nouns.
> **3** We use *much / many* with countable nouns.
> **4** We often use *any, much,* and *many* in **negative / affirmative** sentences.
> **5** We use *some, any,* and *a lot of* with countable and uncountable nouns.

5 Choose the correct words and then answer the quiz with your partner.

1 They don't serve **many / much** ___ in some schools.
   a junk food   **b** healthy food
2 In China they eat **any / a lot of** ___
   a rice.   **b** burgers.
3 Vegetarians don't eat **any / much** ___
   a vegetables.   **b** meat.
4 There aren't **much / many** ___ in a healthy diet.
   a potato chips   **b** apples
5 It's healthy to eat **some / any** ___ each day.
   a fruit   **b** candy

6 ACTIVATE What do you usually eat and drink each week? Complete the sentences. Then compare with other people in the class.

1 I eat some ___.
2 I never eat any ___.
3 I don't eat many ___.
4 I drink a lot of ___.
5 I don't drink much ___.
6 I never drink any ___.

> I eat some fruit and vegetables every day. What about you?

> I don't eat many vegetables, but I eat a lot of fruit.

> **◯** *Finished?*
> **What is a really horrible meal? Describe it.**

Evan	Hey, Molly! Do you want to go to the park after school?
Molly	No. Sorry, Evan, I can't. I have a math test tomorrow.
Evan	Oh, right. That's too bad.
Molly	Yes, I know.
Evan	What about Saturday, then? Are you busy?
Molly	No. Why? What are you doing?
Evan	Some of us are meeting at the shopping mall if you want to come.
Molly	Sounds good. I have to go now. Text me later, OK?
Evan	OK. Bye, Molly.

1 Answer the questions with a partner.

1 Where do you go after school?
2 When and where do you meet your friends?
3 What do you do with your friends?

2 ● 2.23 Listen to the dialogue. Can Molly go to the shopping mall on Saturday?

3 ● 2.24 Complete the dialogue with key phrases. Then listen and check.

> **KEY PHRASES ○ Invitations**
>
> Do you want to go (to the park after school)?
> Are you busy (on Saturday)?
> That's too bad.
> Sounds good.
> What about (Saturday), then?
> No, sorry, (Evan), I can't.

Girl	¹___ this afternoon?
Boy	Yes, I have basketball practice.
Girl	²___ to the movies after school tomorrow?
Boy	³___, Kate, ___. I have a game.
Girl	⁴___. What about Saturday afternoon, then?
Boy	⁵___. Text me later, OK?
Girl	OK. Bye.

4 ● 2.25 Listen to three dialogues. Which questions and answers do you hear?

1 Are you busy this evening?
2 Do you want to go to the movies tomorrow?
3 What about Friday evening, then?
4 What are you doing this weekend?

a I'm going to town with Nelly.
b Yes, I have a lot of homework.
c No, sorry, Ben, I can't.
d Sounds good. Text me later, OK?

5 Work in pairs. Change the words in blue in exercise 4 and make new mini-dialogues. Use the words below or your own ideas. Practice with a partner.

> tomorrow night / a party
> on Saturday / dance class
> tonight / soccer game   later / swimming

> Are you busy tomorrow night?

> Yes, I'm going to a party.

6 ACTIVATE Work in pairs. Prepare a new dialogue using the dialogue in exercise 3 as a model. Use the words in exercise 5 or your own ideas. Practice the new dialogue.

WRITING ◻ An e-mail about school
I can write an e-mail about my school.

5

Delete	Reply	Reply All	Forward	New	Mailboxes	Get Mail

Hi!

1 I'm very happy that you're coming to stay with us next month.

Here's some information about my schedule and my school.

2 School starts at 8:15 and there are six classes every day. The classes are forty-five minutes long. All students study English, math, and science, but we can choose other subjects like geography and Spanish.

3 There are clubs after school, for example drama, table tennis, and music. I go to drama club once a week.

4 I usually have lunch in the cafeteria. It's good because you can buy snack food, such as sandwiches and pizza, but you can also have a salad and a hot meal.

See you next month. Bye for now.
Jackie

1 Read the model text and answer the questions.

  1 Why is she writing the e-mail?
  2 Is the e-mail formal or informal?
  3 Which paragraph is about after-school activities?
  4 Which paragraph is about food?
  5 How many school subjects does she mention?

2 Complete the key phrases for giving information. Then look at the model text and check.

> **KEY PHRASES ◯ Giving information about school**
>
> 1 Here's ___ information ___ ….
> 2 School ___ at (8:15) and ___ (six) classes.
> 3 The ___ are (forty-five minutes) ___.
> 4 ___ students study (English, math, and science), but we ___ choose ….
> 5 There are clubs ___ school.

Language point: Giving examples

3 We use *like*, *for example*, and *such as* to give examples. Find examples of these in the text. Then complete the sentences with your own ideas.

I'm interested in martial arts like *judo and karate.*

  1 She eats a lot of junk food, for example ___.
  2 I prefer subjects like ___.
  3 There are people here from different countries, such as ___.
  4 I eat a lot of fruit and vegetables, for example ___.
  5 Some people do indoor sports like ___.
  6 In the cafeteria you can buy healthy food, such as ___.

4 **ACTIVATE** Follow the steps in the writing guide.

> **◯ WRITING GUIDE**
>
> **A TASK**
>
> A student is visiting your school soon. Write an e-mail and give some information.
>
> **B THINK AND PLAN**
>
> 1 When is the person visiting you?
> 2 What time do classes start?
> 3 How many classes are there every day?
> 4 How long are the classes?
> 5 What subjects do all students do? Which subjects can they choose?
> 6 What extra activities are there after school?
> 7 What do you have for lunch on school days?
>
> **C WRITE**
>
> Paragraph 1: Introduction
> *Here's some information …*
> Paragraph 2: Schedule, subjects, and extra activities
> *School starts at …*
> Paragraph 3: Food
> *I have lunch …*
>
> **D CHECK**
>
> • the greeting and the ending of the e-mail
> • expressions for giving examples
> • spelling

Vocabulary

1 Match the words in the box with the sentences.

> history   P.E.   music   chess   math
> computer science   test   break

1 Tom's playing with the white pieces and Karen with the black.
2 We're studying the 15th century this year.
3 We go to the computer room for this class.
4 Do girls play baseball at your school?
5 We have twenty minutes in the morning.
6 What's 13 x 95?
7 The questions are always very difficult.
8 I play the guitar and the piano.

2 Complete the lists with the words in the box.

> French fries   pears   basketball   class
> juice   Spanish

1 soccer, swimming, ___
2 science, geography, ___
3 homework, subject, ___
4 soda, water, ___
5 hamburgers, potato chips, ___
6 apples, grapes, ___

Language focus

3 Write true sentences with *can* or *can't*.

play tennis
I can't play tennis.
1 swim one kilometer
2 speak Mandarin
3 stand on my hands
4 make pizzas
5 dance salsa
6 eat six hamburgers

4 Write questions and short answers for your sentences in exercise 3.

> *Can you play tennis?*   *No, I can't.*

5 Choose the correct words.

1 I never eat **any** / **some** potato chips.
2 I don't have **much** / **many** rice.
3 There's **much** / **a lot of** salad on my plate.
4 There's **any** / **some** water on the table.
5 Can I have **a** / **some** sandwich, please?
6 I always have lunch at **the** / **a** school cafeteria.
7 I don't eat **much** / **many** pears.
8 I never eat **a lot of** / **some** snacks at school.

Communication

6 Choose the correct responses to the sentences.

1 Can I go out later?
   a Yes, you can.   b Why not?
   c Yes, you are.
2 Sorry, John, I can't come.
   a Sounds good.   b That's too bad.
   c Text me later.
3 How often do you have computer science?
   a At five o'clock.   b Once a week.
   c This afternoon.
4 When do you have history?
   a Twice a week.   b Three hours a week.
   c On Friday mornings.
5 Can I wear jeans to the restaurant?
   a No, you don't.   b No, sorry, you can't.
   c Sounds good.
6 I have a history test this afternoon.
   a Oh dear!   b Cool!   c Why not?

Listening

7 ● 2.26 **Listen to Sally talking about her school lunches. Complete the text.**

We have a self-service cafeteria at my school and the food isn't ¹___. Some students buy ²___ and soda because they don't like the food. But I ³___ eat at school. I think the food is ⁴___ and we can choose the main dish. There is always ⁵___ with pasta or rice and some vegetables. Some of my friends are not very happy because they don't serve many ⁶___. I like French fries, but I don't want to eat them every day! My favorite day is Friday because they always serve ⁷___. I also eat a lot of ⁸___ and there are always pears and apples.

1 Work in groups. Answer the questions.

   1 What do you like about school?

   2 What do you not like?

   3 What would your dream school be like?

2 Read the text. How many of the ideas are the same as yours?

3 Make a poster about your dream school. Follow the steps in the project checklist.

4 Put all of the posters on the wall to make a dream school art gallery. Look at the other posters. Choose the school you like best.

5 Discuss: What could you change in your school to turn it into a dream school?

⬤ PROJECT CHECKLIST

1 Think about your dream school. Write short texts about each of these things:
- the building
- the surroundings
- the classrooms
- the cafeteria
- the people
- the schedule

2 Find some pictures for your poster.

3 Make a poster with your texts and pictures.

Building
The school is in a big and modern building and it's very colorful. It has big windows. It isn't dirty or ugly. There is also a really good gym and a swimming pool.

Classrooms
Every classroom has the latest technology, such as laptops and interactive whiteboards. The students usually speak to students in other countries by webcam.

Cafeteria
The cafeteria is fantastic. You can eat what you want and the food is very healthy. You can eat salads, healthy burgers, and organic French fries.

Surroundings
My dream school is in a park. There are lots of trees, a school garden, and a small zoo. Students can feed and play with the animals.

My dream school

People
The teachers and students are really friendly and like going to school. The teachers aren't boring.

Schedule
Each day starts at 10:00. The classes are always interesting and students can study any subject they like, for example music, art, dance, or sports. It isn't a problem if you get bad grades.

Names and places

Start thinking

1 Who was Alfred Nobel?
2 Which names are popular for children in the U.S.?
3 What do you know about Nashville?

Aims

Communication: I can ...

- talk about jobs.
- understand an article about the history of names.
- talk about the past with *was* and *were*.
- understand an interview about how people named some American towns.
- talk about my past experiences.
- talk about my weekend.
- write about a place and its history.

Vocabulary

- Jobs
- Regular verbs

Language focus

- *was* and *were*
- *there was* and *there were*
- Simple past of regular verbs
- Past time expressions

Reach Out Options

Extra listening and speaking
Talking about a movie or TV program
 Page 93

Curriculum extra
Language and literature: Myths and legends
⇒ Page 101

Culture
Roman Britain
⇒ Page 109

Vocabulary puzzles
Jobs; Regular verbs
⇒ Page 117

VOCABULARY ■ Jobs
I can talk about jobs.

1 Do *The Name Quiz* on page 59. Complete the descriptions of the people with words in the box. Then add vowels to complete the words in blue.

> inventor   firefighter   explorer   writer   actor   farmer
> waiter / waitress   chef   scientist   artist   musician
> doctor   teacher   nurse   mechanic
> construction worker   king   queen   hairdresser
> businessman / businesswoman

2 🔊 2.32 Listen and check your answers. Do we use *a* and *an* with jobs in English?

3 Look at the adjectives in the box. Which words can you use to describe the jobs in exercise 1?

> boring   interesting   easy   difficult   stressful
> dangerous   hard   well-paid   tiring   exciting

4 🔊 2.33 Look at the key phrases. Which phrases can you complete with a job? Which phrases can you complete with a word in exercise 3? Listen and check.

> **KEY PHRASES ◯ Talking about jobs**
>
> 1 I want to be a / an ___.
> 2 He / She is a / an ___.
> 3 I think being a / an ___ is ___.
> 4 It's a / an ___ job.
> 5 A / An ___ works in a / an hospital / garage / restaurant / office / school / theater.

5 🔊 2.34 Read the descriptions and guess the jobs. Then listen and check. Do you agree with the descriptions?

1 She works in a hospital. It's a hard job. She's a ___.
2 He works in a garage. It's a hard job. He's a ___.
3 She works in an office. It's a well-paid job. She's a ___.
4 She works in a restaurant. It's a tiring job. She's a ___.
5 He works in a school. It's a stressful job. He's a ___.
6 He works in many places. It's a dangerous job. He's a ___.

6 **ACTIVATE** Work in pairs. Ask and answer questions about jobs. Use the key phrases and the words in exercise 3.

> What do you want to be?
>
> I want to be ... . I think it's ... .
>
> Yes, but it's ... .
>
> What is your ... ?
>
> He's a / an ... . He works in ... .

> ◯ *Finished?*
> **What do you want to be? Why? Write sentences about your dream job.**

The Name Quiz

1 Alfred Nobel was a scientist and an *inventor* from Sweden. We use his name for the Nobel Prize.

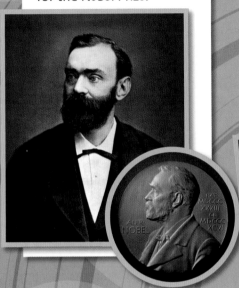

2 Levi Strauss was a ___ in America. We use his name for L __ v __ 's j __ __ ns.

3 Antoine-Joseph Sax was a ___ from Belgium. We use his name for the s __ x __ ph __ n __.

4 Amerigo Vespucci was an ___ from Italy. We use his name for __ m __ r __ c __.

5 Marie Curie was a ___ from Poland. We use her name for the element c __ r __ __ m.

7 Klaus Maertens was a ___ from Germany. We use his name for D __ c M __ rt __ ns b __ __ ts.

6 Margherita of Savoy was a ___ of Italy. We use her name for Margherita p __ zz __.

EXCUSE ME?
WHAT'S YOUR NAME?

Where do first and last names come from? American and British names are very similar because many Americans were originally from England. Let's look at the history of names in both England and the U.S.

1 ___ First names were important in England in the 11th century. The population was small and most people lived in villages. Last names weren't necessary because there weren't many people. When the French King William I invaded England in 1066, he wasn't happy with this. In his opinion, people needed last names.

2 ___ In those days, there were different ways to choose a last name: some people used their job (Baker, Cook), some used places (Hill, Wood), and some used their nickname (Short, Brown) or the name of a parent (Johnson = son of John).

3 ___ These old last names are common in modern Britain and the U.S., but many first names are different. There is nothing new about naming a child after a famous person, but the type of celebrity is different today. In the past, the names of kings, queens, scientists, artists, or writers were fashionable.

4 ___ Many parents today name their children after pop stars, sports stars, or movie stars like Justin, Keira, Brad, and Lebron. They do this because they are fans of these celebrities. After Barack Obama became president of the U.S. in 2008, many people named their sons Barack and their girls after his wife and daughters: Michelle, Malia, and Sasha. One British soccer fan named his baby after the Manchester United team. His son has a first name and ten middle names!

5 ___ Other parents want their children to have original first names and they sometimes choose the brand names of products. One year there were 298 Armanis, 49 Canons, 5 Jaguars, 1 Xerox, and 353 girls named Lexus.

1 What are popular names for children in your country? Are there many unusual names?

2 🔵 2.35 Read the text and match headings a–f with paragraphs 1–5. There is one heading that you do not need. Listen and check.

a The English choose their last names
b Fans and stars
c What? No last name?
d Popular French last names
e Is it a baby or a car?
f First names of the past

3 Read the text again and write *true* or *false*. Correct the false sentences.

1 You can have lots of middle names in Britain.
2 Some children have brand names for names.
3 Last names were necessary in England before the 11th century.
4 Brown and Short were nicknames in the past.
5 Many parents named their children after singers in the past.

4 **BUILD YOUR VOCABULARY** Translate the words in blue. Ask and answer the questions.

1 What is your first name?
2 Do you have any middle names?
3 Do you and your friends have nicknames?
4 Do you know the meaning of your last name?
5 What brand names do you like?

5 **ABOUT YOU** Ask and answer the questions.

1 What are your favorite first names?
2 What are common last names in your country?
3 What do you think of brand names and celebrity names for children?

KEIRA

CANON

JAGUAR

LEBRON

LANGUAGE FOCUS ◼ *was, were* • *there was, there were*
I can talk about the past with *was* and *were*.

6

was, were

1 Complete the sentences from the text on page 60. Then read rules 1–3.

First names ¹___ important in the 11th century.
The population ²___ small.
Last names ³___ necessary.
King William I ⁴___ happy with this.

⭕ RULES

1 We use *was* / *were* to talk about the past.
2 *Was* / *Were* are the past forms of *be*.
3 We form the negative with *was* / *were* + *not*.

2 Complete the questions and answers with *was*, *were*, *wasn't*, and *weren't*. Then answer questions 1–2.

Was I late yesterday? Yes, you ¹___.
²___ Tom here yesterday? No, he ³___.
⁴___ you tired last night? Yes, I ⁵___.
Were they at school yesterday? No, they ⁶___.

1 In questions, is *was* / *were* before or after the pronoun / noun?
2 In short answers, is *was* / *were* before or after the pronoun?

(More practice ⇨ Workbook page 49)

3 Write affirmative and negative sentences. Then ask and answer with a partner using short answers.

Shakespeare (teacher / writer)
Shakespeare wasn't a teacher. He was a writer.
1 William Boeing (plane / engineer)
2 The Beatles (insects / musicians)
3 Henry Ford (car / inventor)
4 Marie and Pierre Curie (explorers / scientists)
5 Bach and Mozart (writers / musicians)
6 Queen Margherita (pizza / person)
7 The *Titanic* (village / ship)
8 Picasso and Van Gogh (actors / artists)

there was, there were

4 Complete the table.

	Affirmative	Negative
Singular	There was a king.	¹___ any food.
Plural	²___ a lot of villages.	There weren't many people.

(More practice ⇨ Workbook page 49)

5 Complete the sentences with *there was / wasn't* or *there were / weren't*.

In the 11th century, …
1 ___ a French king called William.
2 ___ any cars.
3 ___ any shopping malls in England.
4 ___ a lot of kings and queens.
5 ___ a computer in every house.
6 ___ a lot of small villages.

6 ACTIVATE Complete questions 1–8 using the words in the box and *was* or *were*. Then ask and answer the questions with a partner.

(What   Where   Who   When)

1 ___ your favorite primary school teachers?
2 ___ the last time you were at a party?
3 ___ your favorite TV programs last year?
4 ___ the last place you were on vacation?
5 ___ your last meal?
6 ___ the last shopping mall you were in?
7 ___ your favorite day last week?
8 ___ popular singers last year?

⭕ *Finished?*
Write five sentences about things that are different today and a hundred years ago.
Today there are a lot of cell phones.
There weren't any cell phones a hundred years ago.

Was Shakespeare a teacher?

No, he wasn't.

Strange Town, U.S.

KPRQ Radio, Friday, 8:00 p.m.

Chicken, Why, Experiment, Yellow, Santa Claus, Jupiter, Gas, Frankenstein, Sandwich, Pray, Tarzan, Moon, Disco, Paradise, War.

A strange collection of words, but they all have one thing in common. They are the names of places in the U.S. Find out more about strange place names on Friday's program.

1 Complete the sentences with the verbs in the box. Do the sentences refer to the past or the present?

> invaded   named   invented   crossed
> changed   discovered   stopped
> traveled

1 Alexander Graham Bell ___ the telephone.
2 Thomas Mapother IV ___ his name to Tom Cruise.
3 The Romans ___ France in 58 BC.
4 Americans first ___ gold in the U.S. in 1799.
5 Marco Polo ___ to China in the 13th century.
6 Columbus ___ the Atlantic Ocean in 1492.
7 They ___ their baby after a pop star.
8 The bus ___ in Los Angeles.

2 Study the spelling rules. Then complete the table with the verbs in exercise 1.

Spelling rules: Simple past		
→ + -ed	→ e + -d	double final consonant + -ed
listen → listened	name → named	prefer → preferred

> **Pronunciation: Past tense -ed endings**
> ⇨ Workbook page 92

STUDY STRATEGY ○ Multiple choice listening

3 Prepare to listen. Read the questions in exercise 4 carefully. Which towns are you going to hear about? Are there any answers which you can guess now?

4 ● 2.36 Read the information about Strange Town and listen to the program. Choose the correct answers. Then listen again and check.

1 New Amsterdam changed to New York because ___
   a people traveled there from York.
   b the British invaded it and named it after the Duke of York.
   c people didn't like the original name.
2 Why is Why called Why?
   a Because people there ask a lot of questions.
   b Because it is on the River Why.
   c Because the road is in the shape of a Y.
3 People named their town Happy because ___
   a they discovered gold there.
   b they discovered water there.
   c happy people established it.
4 Is Hell a nice place?
   a Yes, but in the past the river there was dangerous to cross.
   b No, a lot of criminals lived there in the past.
   c It's a nice town, but it is very hot there.

5 ACTIVATE Work in groups. Think of six towns or cities in your country. Where do their names come from? Which names are strange? Compare your ideas.

Simple past of regular verbs

1 Study the sentences and the words in blue. Which sentences refer to the present and which refer to the past? How do you know?

   a I live in New York now.
   b We lived in London in 2009.
   c Wayne plays soccer every Friday.
   d Wayne didn't play soccer last week.

2 Read and complete the rules.

> **○ RULES**
>
> **1** To form the simple past of regular verbs we add ¹___ / -ed to the verb.
> **2** We use *didn't* + verb in the ²___ form.

(More practice ⇨ Workbook page 51)

3 Write affirmative sentences using the simple past. Are they true or false? Correct the false sentences with your partner.

Neil Armstrong (discover) America.
Neil Armstrong discovered America. False.

   1 Europeans ___ (explore) Africa in the 18th century.
   2 Tutankhamen ___ (live) in Egypt a long time ago.
   3 The first astronauts ___ (visit) space in 1981.
   4 Columbus ___ (arrive) in South America about 500 years ago.
   5 People ___ (stop) using horses for transportation in the 19th century.
   6 In 1700, people ___ (travel) by plane.
   7 Alexander Graham Bell ___ (invent) the telephone.

4 Complete the text with affirmative and negative forms of the verbs in parentheses.

CHRISTOPHER COLUMBUS

Columbus **wanted** (want) to find a new way to India. In 1492, he ¹___ (travel) across the Atlantic Ocean. He ²___ (arrive) in San Salvador in the Bahamas two months later. He ³___ (visit) a lot of islands and he ⁴___ (name) them the Indies. He ⁵___ (call) the native people Indians. It was a very beautiful place, but he ⁶___ (not discover) any gold there. Columbus ⁷___ (not stay) a long time and he ⁸___ (arrive) back in Spain in March 1493. The King and Queen of Spain weren't happy because he ⁹___ (not discover) any gold or a new way to India. Columbus ¹⁰___ (not visit) North America, but he was the first European to explore Central America.

Past time expressions

5 Study the key phrases. How many similar phrases can you find in the sentences in exercises 3 and 4? What is the position of *ago* in a time expression?

> **KEY PHRASES ○ Past time expressions**
>
> last week / month / year / weekend / Saturday
> two days / three weeks / 500 years ago
> in the 18th century
> in 1961 / March 1493
> yesterday

(More practice ⇨ Workbook page 51)

6 **ACTIVATE** Talk about your experiences with a partner. Use the time expressions in the box and your own ideas.

> about ten minutes ago   yesterday
> last weekend   in 2009   a month ago
> in the 20th century   last month
> an hour ago   last summer

> I visited my grandparents last weekend. What about you?

> I visited my grandparents a month ago.

> **○ *Finished?***
> Write the past forms of the verbs in the box. Then write sentences using the key phrases in exercise 5.
>
> watch jump climb attack finish dance

Bella	Hi, Ethan. How was your weekend?
Ethan	Great, thanks. I ¹___ my uncle and then I ²___ to New York.
Bella	Really? Were you on your own?
Ethan	No. I was with my cousin. She knows the city very well.
Bella	What was New York like?
Ethan	It was cool. The stores ³___ amazing.
Bella	Only the stores?
Ethan	No, ⁴___ were a lot of things to do. My favorite place ⁵___ Central Park.
Bella	What about the tourist sites?
Ethan	I wanted to visit the Metropolitan Museum of Art, but there ⁶___ time. And how about you? Was your weekend good?
Bella	Yeah, it was great. There was a party at Jon's house on Saturday night.
Ethan	Sounds good.

1 Look at the picture. Ethan is returning from a trip to New York. What places in New York do you think he is talking about?

2 ● 2.37 Complete the dialogue. Then listen and check. Was your answer in exercise 1 correct?

> there   was   were   traveled   visited
> wasn't

3 ● 2.38 Listen to the key phrases 1–4 and reply with the correct responses a–d. Then practice the dialogue.

KEY PHRASES ○ Talking about the weekend

1 How was your weekend?
2 Were you on your own?
3 What was (New York) like?
4 Was your weekend good?

a No. I was with (my cousin).
b Yeah, it was great.
c Great, thanks.
d It was cool.

4 ● 2.39 Look at the tables and listen to three short conversations. Which questions and answers do you hear?

Questions		
How was	your weekend? the trip? the movie?	
What was	your vacation the game the party	like?

Answers		
It was	great! cool. OK. terrible!	
The special effects The story The food Barcelona The people The places The weather	was were wasn't weren't	really interesting. very nice. really good. really bad. awful terrible.

5 Work with a partner. Practice different questions and answers.

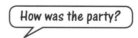

> How was the party?

> It was terrible! The food was awful.

6 **ACTIVATE** Work in pairs. Prepare a new dialogue using the dialogue in exercise 2 as a model. Change the words in blue. Use the phrases in exercise 4 and your own ideas. Practice the new dialogue.

WRITING ● An article about a town
I can write about a place and its history.

6

History in the streets – Nashville

1. Nashville is a city in the north of the state of Tennessee, in the U.S. It's on the Cumberland River and near Memphis and Atlanta, other big American cities.

2. People first lived in Nashville in 1779, about 230 years ago. In those days, its name was Fort Nashborough and it wasn't very big. In 1850, about 11,000 people lived there. Today the population is over 600,000.

3. There are lots of interesting places to visit in Nashville, many related to music. Nashville is called "The Music City" because lots of famous country musicians sing there. Tourists can hear good music at The Grand Ole Opry or the Ryman Auditorium.

4. The people of Nashville are called Nashvillians. Famous people from Nashville include Kitty Wells and Miley Cyrus. Kitty Wells was a famous musician in the 1950s and 1960s, and Miley Cyrus is an actress and singer who became famous in the 2000s.

1 Read the model text. Match paragraphs 1–4 with topics a–d.

   a Places   b People
   c History   d Location

2 Read the model text again and answer the questions.

   1 What river is Nashville on?
   2 What was Nashville's name 230 years ago?
   3 What was its population in 1850?
   4 Why is Nashville called "The Music City"?

3 Study the key phrases. Match the key phrases with paragraphs 1–4.

> **KEY PHRASES ◯ City history**
>
> … is a city in the (north) of … .
> Today the population is … .
> It's on …   It's near … .
> In those days, its name was … .
> The people of … are called … .
> People first lived in … .
> Famous (people from) … include … .

4 Work in pairs. Use the key phrases to make sentences about a city you know.

Language point: Time expressions

5 Match phrases 1–5 with time expressions a–e.

   1 Kitty Wells was popular
   2 Nashville had a population of 11,000
   3 Nashville is a big city
   4 People first lived in Nashville about
   5 Miley Cyrus started singing

   a in 1850.
   b in the 2000s.
   c in the 1950s and 1960s.
   d 230 years ago.
   e today.

6 **ACTIVATE** Follow the steps in the writing guide.

> ### Notes – Miami
>
> a Location: south of the U.S., in the state of Florida
> b Name: Biscayne Bay Country (120 years ago)
> c Population: 1,700 one hundred and ten years ago, about 400,000 now
> d Street names: Ocean Drive (historic buildings, Art Deco hotels)
> e People: Miamians
> f Famous Miamians: Gloria Estefan (singer known as "Queen of Latin Pop"), Eva Mendes (actress), and Anna Kournikova (tennis player)

> **◯ WRITING GUIDE**
>
> **A TASK**
>
> Write an article about a town of your choice or use the notes about Miami.
>
> **B THINK AND PLAN**
>
> Read the model text again. How many paragraphs are there?
>
> Read the notes a–f about Miami. What information do you want to put in each paragraph of your article?
> **Paragraph 1: a, …**
>
> **C WRITE**
>
> Write your article and follow your paragraph plan. Look at the model text to help you. Use the key phrases and time expressions.
>
> **D CHECK**
>
> • position and spelling of the time expressions

Vocabulary

1 Reorder the letters and write the jobs.

1	rswiatse	waitress	6	rensu	___
2	marfer	___	7	cotdro	___
3	erwitr	___	8	gfeferihirt	___
4	hefc	___	9	hemcncia	___
5	ortac	___	10	iesncitst	___

2 Choose the correct words.

1 Columbus **discovered** / **invented** America.
2 My grandmother changed her **last name** / **first name** when she got married.
3 We went to New York two weeks **before** / **ago**.
4 Tom is a **chef** / **mechanic** and he works in a restaurant.
5 William I was **King** / **Queen** of England 1,000 years ago.
6 Being a firefighter is a **boring** / **dangerous** job.
7 Victoria was a popular first name in the 19th **century** / **ago**.
8 Jaguar is a famous **brand name** / **nickname** for a car.

Language focus

3 Complete the dialogue with the affirmative or negative form of *was* and *were*.

Jen **Were** you at the party on Saturday?
Paul Yes, I ¹___.
Jen ²___ any of our friends there?
Paul Yes, I ³___ with Wayne and Cristiano, but Keira and Justin ⁴___ at the party.
Jen ⁵___ it good?
Paul No, it ⁶___. I was very hungry because there ⁷___ any food. And there ⁸___ some very strange people. There ⁹___ one girl called Jaguar and another called Porsche.
Jen Ooh! ¹⁰___ they rich?
Paul No, they ¹¹___. And there ¹²___ two brothers called Xerox. It was incredible – they ¹³___ identical.

4 Write affirmative and negative sentences using the simple past.

I / visit / Trafalgar Square
I visited Trafalgar Square.
Columbus / not discover / North America
Columbus didn't discover North America.

1 we / move / to Miami last year
2 my mom / not change / her name / when she got married
3 we / stay / in Los Angeles last Saturday night
4 John Logie Baird / invent / the TV
5 my dad / stop / smoking / last month
6 my birthday present / not arrive / in the mail this morning

5 Write questions and short answers for the sentences in exercise 4.

Did you visit the Walk of Fame? Yes, I did.
Did Columbus discover North America? No, he didn't.

Communication

6 Match questions 1–8 with answers a–h.

1 What was Chicago like?
2 I want to be a teacher.
3 When did Europeans first visit America?
4 How was the game?
5 Was the weather good?
6 Who was Picasso?
7 Were you on your own?
8 Were there a lot of people?

a No, I was with Rebecca.
b A Spanish artist.
c Yes, there were.
d It was cool. There were a lot of museums.
e Really? I think it's a stressful job.
f Terrible. We lost.
g In the 15th century.
h No, it rained all day.

Listening

7 🔴 2.40 **Listen to a conversation about a trip to Boston. Write *true* or *false*.**

1 Tom visited Boston with his friend Lynne.
2 Faneuil Hall is about 270 years old.
3 Boston was a small town in the 17th century.
4 Boston was important during the American Revolution.
5 It was an important education center.
6 They named the town Boston in the 18th century.
7 Tom didn't visit the park when he was in Boston.

Listening

1 Look at the pictures. Which of the places in the box are not in the pictures?

> river café library school downtown supermarket university

2 ● 2.41 Listen to a conversation. Which place in the pictures is not in Cambridge?

3 ● 2.41 Listen again and complete the sentences.

1 Harvard University is almost ___ years old.
2 The U.S. ___ John F. Kennedy was a student there.
3 There are more than ___ books in the library.
4 Jon's favorite subject is ___.
5 Lucy likes ___ and ___.
6 Lucy played ___ on Sunday.
7 Lucy can't go out because she has a lot of ___ homework.
8 They serve good ___ and ___ at the new café on First Street.

Speaking

4 Work in pairs and prepare a conversation. Imagine one person (A) visited an interesting place in your country last weekend. The other person (B) stayed at home. Make notes about:

- the name of the place and how old it is
- what the place is like and other information (buildings, history, famous people)
- what you liked about it
- who you were with
- student B's weekend.

5 Have a conversation. Use your ideas in exercise 4 and the chart below to help you. One of you is A, one of you is B. Change roles.

A How was your weekend?

B Reply.

A What was it like?

B Reply. *I visited ... . I liked ... .*

A Was it interesting / fun ... ?

B Reply.

A How old is [the place]?

B Reply.

A Were you on your own?

B Reply. *Was your weekend good?*

A Reply. *I ... on Saturday. On Sunday, I ...*

Writing

6 Write a postcard to a friend. Tell your friend about a place you visited last weekend. You can write about Cambridge or the place you talked about in exercise 5. Begin like this:

Dear ...,
Last weekend, I visited ... . It's a ... in the north / south / east / west of ... . It's a really interesting ... . I visited ... .

Games

Start thinking

1 When and where were the first Olympic Games?
2 What is an avatar?
3 Where is Cristiano Ronaldo from?

Aims

Communication: I can ...

- talk about sports and sports events.
- understand an article about video games.
- talk about actions in the past.
- describe people's appearance.
- ask and answer questions about last weekend.
- talk about things I did last weekend.
- write a profile of a famous athlete.

Vocabulary

- Sports
- Describing people

Language focus

- Simple past: regular and irregular verbs
- Simple past: questions
- *also*

Reach Out Options

Extra listening and speaking
Talking about video games
⟹ Page 94

Curriculum extra
Technology: The Internet
⟹ Page 102

Culture
America's favorite games
⟹ Page 110

Vocabulary puzzles
Sports; Describing people
⟹ Page 118

VOCABULARY ◼ Sports
I can talk about sports and sports events.

1 Check the meaning of verbs 1–8. Match these verbs with their past forms in blue in the *Time Traveler Game* on page 69.

1 break ＿＿ 3 run ＿＿ 5 win ＿＿ 7 beat ＿＿
2 score ＿＿ 4 take part ＿＿ 6 play ＿＿ 8 lose ＿＿

2 ● 3.02 Complete the key phrases with the words in the box. Then listen and check. Practice saying the phrases.

> think   answer   right   agree   sure   don't

KEY PHRASES ⭕ Comparing answers

1 I think the ＿＿ is (b).
2 I'm not ＿＿. Maybe it's (c).
3 Yes, I ＿＿.
4 I don't ＿＿ so. I think the answer is (a).
5 Yes, you're ＿＿.
6 I ＿＿ agree.

3 ● 3.03 Read the rules on page 69. Then play the game in teams. Use the key phrases to compare your answers. Then listen and check.

> I think the answer to the first question is c.

> I don't agree. The Vancouver Olympics were in the winter. I think the answer is b.

4 Match the verbs in A with the phrases in B to make collocations about sports. Check your answers in the *Time Traveler Game*.

A		B	
break	win	in a competition	a race
score	play	a race	someone at a game
run	beat	a goal	a record
take part	lose	a game	

5 Find nine of these sports and games in the photos on page 69.

> bike riding   swimming   hockey   skiing   volleyball
> skateboarding   auto racing   chess   tennis
> track and field   golf   soccer   football

6 ACTIVATE Complete the sentences about sports for you. Then talk about your answers with a partner.

1 I'm / I'm not good at ＿＿.
2 I don't take part in ＿＿ competitions because ＿＿.
3 I like / don't like watching ＿＿ on TV.
4 I can / can't beat my friend at ＿＿.
5 I like / don't like playing team games because ＿＿.
6 I enjoy / don't enjoy running a race.

> I'm good at tennis and soccer. What about you?

TIME TRAVELER GAME

Rules Talk about the questions and decide your answers. Then listen to the correct answers. Your team starts with three lives. Each time you get an answer wrong, you lose a life. If you don't have any lives, you are out of the game. The winner is the team with the most lives.

START

1 You took part in a competition in the Vancouver Olympic Games in Canada in 2010. You were on your country's _____ team.
a basketball
b hockey
c table tennis

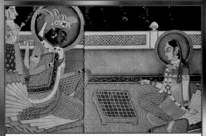

2 You were in _____ in 1903 when the first Tour de France bike race took place.
a London
b Rome
c Paris

3 You ran a race at the first ancient Olympic Games in Greece. They were in _____.
a 776 BC
b AD 776
c AD 1796

6 In _____, you played a new game in the 6th century. You lost the game. It was chess.
a India
b China
c Spain

5 You were at the Olympic Games in 2008. Michael Phelps won _____ medals and broke seven world records.
a eight gold
b eight silver
c four gold and four silver

4 You saw Pelé play soccer in Brazil. He scored _____ goals for his country.
a 170
b 17
c 77

7 A team called the Green Bay Packers won the first Super Bowl in 1967. What is the name of the Super Bowl sport?
a rugby
b football
c bowling

8 You took part in the skateboarding competition at the first X-Games in the U.S. It was in _____.
a 1965
b 1995
c 2005

9 You met King Henry VIII of England. He beat you at a new game called _____.
a squash
b tennis
c golf

FINISH

🔲 *Finished?*
Write two more questions for the *Time Traveler Game*.
You watched Usain Bolt break the world record for 100 m and 200 m ...

Game on!

Big numbers!

Video games and consoles are big business.
¹___. A team of designers took three years to make the Wii console. In its first six months in Europe, people bought 6 million of them. Companies sold the first games in the 1970s and one of the first big video heroes was Mario in the 1980s. *Super Mario World* was the world's number one game in the 1990s and 20 million people bought it.

War and peace

In the early years, many people thought that video games were boys' toys because companies sold most of their games to men. The designers created a lot of violent action games and women didn't like them. ²___. Then in 2000, games creator Will Wright made the *SIMS* game. In the *SIMS* game, players designed houses and built towns. ³___.

Too much?

Today, video games are popular with all ages and there's a lot of choice. But games can cause health problems, especially when people play for hours. Many children prefer video games to sports and they become overweight. ⁴___. Video games are good for your imagination and memory. And they are also great entertainment. So enjoy playing video games, but remember to do other activities, too!

1 Do you know the video games in the photos?

2 ● 3.04 Read the text and complete gaps 1–4 with sentences a–e. There is one sentence that you do not need. Listen and check.

a But there are some positive things, too.
b They preferred creative games.
c They don't do a lot of sports.
d Today, companies sell more than 100 million games a year.
e It soon became the number one game of all time with both men and women.

3 BUILD YOUR VOCABULARY Find the nouns for these verbs in the article. Then complete the sentences.

> create   design   play   entertain
> imagine   choose   remember

1 Video game ___s make very violent games.
2 Shigeru Miyamoto was the ___ of Mario.
3 My favorite form of ___ is TV.
4 There is a large ___ of books in the library.
5 My favorite soccer ___ is Lionel Messi.
6 You use your ___ when you write a story.
7 He has a good ___. He never forgets.

4 ABOUT YOU Ask and answer the questions.

1 Do you play games? Why / Why not?
2 What games do your friends play?
3 Why do you think games are popular?
4 What games do boys and girls like?
5 What can you learn from video games?

LANGUAGE FOCUS ■ **Simple past: regular and irregular verbs**
I can talk about actions in the past.

 7

1 Look at the forms of *play* and *make* in the sentences. Which verb is regular? How do you know?

1 He **played** violent games.
2 We **didn't play** creative games.
3 He **made** creative games.
4 You **didn't make** violent games.

More practice ⇨ Workbook page 57

2 Find the simple past forms of these verbs in the article on page 70. Complete the table.

~~sell~~ buy ~~design~~ become think
prefer create build take

Regular verbs	Irregular verbs
design – designed	sell – sold

STUDY STRATEGY ○ **Using the Workbook irregular verbs list**

3 Study the irregular verbs list on page 104 in your Workbook and test your partner.

What's the past of "have"?   It's "had".

4 Make affirmative and negative sentences. Use the prompts and your own ideas. Then compare your answers with a partner.

I / buy / a game.
I didn't buy a game. I bought a CD.
What about you? I bought a book.

1 I / have / a sandwich for lunch.
2 I / meet / my friend in town.
3 we / go / to a restaurant.
4 I / read / a book in bed.
5 we / eat / at home on Friday.
6 I / write / a letter to a friend.

5 Complete the text with the correct simple past form of the verbs in the boxes.

Game master

not like   win   play   not listen   know

When Johnathan Wendel was thirteen, he often went to arcades and he ¹___ games against older teenagers. He was very good and he often ²___. His parents ³___ about this, but they ⁴___ it. Luckily, Johnathan ⁵___ to them.

not win   become   take   be

When he was eighteen, he ⁶___ part in his first professional competition. He ⁷___ but he ⁸___ third. In his next competition, he ⁹___ champion of the game, *Quake 3*.

start   make   not lose   beat   travel

After that, he ¹⁰___ around the world and he ¹¹___ very often. He ¹²___ all the best players. He ¹³___ his company Fatal1ty, Inc. and ¹⁴___ a lot of money selling things for computers.

6 **ACTIVATE** Play a true and false game. Order the time expressions in the box. Follow the instructions. Start with the most recent.

- Write true and false sentences about your past activities using the time expressions and verbs from the class.
- Read them out to your partner.
- Can your partner guess which are true and which are false?

this morning   yesterday   last night
on Saturday   on the weekend   last year
when I was young   two weeks ago
an hour ago

I met a famous actor on vacation last year.

False.

No, it's true!

1 Complete 1–5 in the avatar guide with the words in the box.

> mustache   dark   curly   ~~tall~~   blue   slim

CREATE YOUR AVATAR □□□

Height

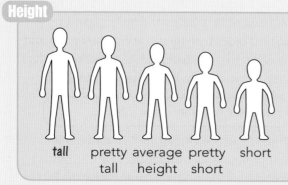

| tall | pretty tall | average height | pretty short | short |

Build

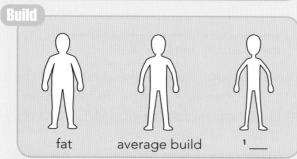

| fat | average build | ¹ ___ |

Hair

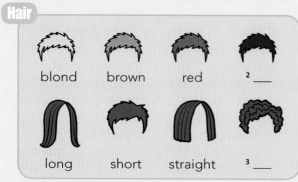

| blond | brown | red | ² ___ |

| long | short | straight | ³ ___ |

Eye color

| green | ⁴ ___ | brown |

Other features

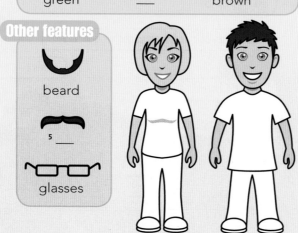

beard

⁵ ___

glasses

2 Complete the descriptions with words in exercise 1.

1 She's average height and average build. She has ___ eyes and ___ blond hair.
2 He's ___ and slim. He has ___ dark hair.
3 She's fat and pretty ___. She has purple hair and she's wearing ___.
4 He's very short and ___. He has a beard and a ___.

3 🔊 3.05 Read the introduction to *Last Coffee at the Corner Café*. Then listen to the interview.

Last Coffee at the Corner Café

Notes: Agent Koji had breakfast at the Corner Café at 8:00 yesterday morning. At 9:10 he died, after drinking coffee with poison in it. Detective Lambert talked to the waitress, Larna Scott.

4 🔊 3.05 Listen again and answer the questions. Who was the murderer?

1 Did the woman with blond hair speak to Koji?
2 Where did this woman sit?
3 Did she leave at eight o'clock?
4 Who did the man with a beard talk to?
5 Was the short woman with a friend?
6 What did the woman buy?
7 Did a man with long dark hair speak to Koji?
8 Did the detective have coffee?

5 ACTIVATE Invent a new character using the words in exercise 1. Listen to your partner's description and draw his or her character.

My avatar is a woman. She's tall and ...

LANGUAGE FOCUS ◼ **Simple past: questions**
I can ask and answer questions about last weekend.

7

1 Complete the questions from exercise 4 on page 72.

1 Did the woman with blond hair ___ to Koji?
2 Where ___ this woman sit?
3 ___ a man with long dark hair speak to Koji?
4 Did the detective ___ coffee?

2 Can you remember the answers to the questions in exercise 1? Match them with the answers a–d. Then complete the rules.

a No, she didn't.
b No, he didn't.
c Yes, he did.
d By the window.

⊙ **RULES**

1 We make simple past questions with ¹___ + noun / pronoun + verb.
2 We make short answers with Yes, / ²___ + pronoun + did / ³___.

(More practice ⇨ Workbook page 59)

3 Write questions in the simple past. Then ask and answer with your partner.

drink coffee for breakfast

(**Did you drink coffee for breakfast?**)

(**Yes, I did. / No, I didn't.**)

1 read a book in bed
2 buy clothes last weekend
3 come to school on the bus this morning
4 go to bed early
5 have a lot of homework last night
6 eat candy yesterday
7 use a computer at school
8 call a friend

(Pronunciation: Diphthongs: /eɪ/, /aɪ/, /oʊ/, /aʊ/
⇨ Workbook page 92)

4 Complete the questions and answers in the dialogue. Use the question words in the box and the past tense of the verbs in parentheses.

(How   What   What time   Who   Where)

A ¹___ did Koji come into the café?
B He ²___ into the café at 8:00. (come)
A ³___ did he sit?
B He ⁴___ near the door. (sit)
A ⁵___ did he talk to?
B He ⁶___ to a man with a beard. (talk)
A ⁷___ did Koji drink?
B He ⁸___ coffee. (drink)
A ⁹___ did he die?
B He ¹⁰___ after drinking the coffee. (die)

5 Complete the questions about last weekend with the simple past form of the verbs.

1 Where ___ (you / go) on Saturday?
2 ___ (you / meet) any friends at the shopping mall?
3 What ___ (you / watch) on TV?
4 ___ (you / call) anyone?
5 When ___ (you / do) your homework?
6 ___ (you / play) any video games?
7 Who ___ (you / see) on Sunday?
8 What time ___ (you / go) to bed?

6 **ACTIVATE** Speak about last weekend with your partner. Ask and answer the questions in exercise 5. How many things did you both do?

(**Where did you go on Saturday?**)

(**I went to the movies.**)

(**Me too!**)

⊙ *Finished?*
Write sentences about your memories of when you were young.
I remember that we went to Argentina on vacation when I was three.

Tyler	Hi, Megan. Did you have a good weekend?
Megan	It was OK. I bought a new game. I played it all weekend.
Tyler	You played a video game all weekend?
Megan	¹___
Tyler	We went to the game on Saturday.
Megan	²___
Tyler	Yeah. Why don't you come with us next time?
Megan	³___
Tyler	We had a barbecue on Sunday.
Megan	How was it?
Tyler	⁴___

1 Think about last weekend. What did you do? Did you have a good weekend?

2 ● 3.06 Complete the dialogue with sentences a–d. Then listen and check.

a OK. Why not? Did you do anything else?
b That's cool. Was it good?
c It was terrible. It rained!
d Yeah. What about you? What did you do?

3 ● 3.07 Listen to the intonation. Is the speaker interested or bored? Listen and repeat the sentences.

1 It was OK.
2 I played a video game.
3 We watched TV all weekend.
4 It was great.
5 I went shopping with my mom and dad.
6 We had a party.

4 Complete the table with the activities in the box. Then add your own ideas.

> ~~have a party~~   go to a soccer game
> watch TV   go shopping with friends
> ~~go shopping with mom and dad~~
> visit a museum   have a barbecue
> do homework   watch a DVD
> read a book   go to a theme park

Interesting activities	Boring activities
have a party	go shopping with mom and dad

5 Study the key phrases. Which responses are positive?

KEY PHRASES ○ Asking about the weekend

Questions	Responses
Did you have a good weekend?	It was great.
	It was OK.
What about you?	It was boring.
What did you do?	Yeah. Fantastic!
How was it?	It was terrible.
Was it good?	Not really.

6 ACTIVATE Work in pairs. Prepare a new dialogue using the dialogue in exercise 2 as a model. Use the key phrases in exercise 5 and activities in exercise 4 or your own ideas. Practice the new dialogue.

> Did you have a good weekend?

> Not really. I went shopping with my mom and dad on Saturday.

> What did you do on Sunday?

> Nothing. What about you?

> I went to a theme park on Saturday.

WRITING ● A profile
I can write a profile of a famous athlete.

7

Star player: Cristiano Ronaldo

1 Cristiano Ronaldo's full name is Cristiano Ronaldo dos Santos Aveiro. He was born on February 5, 1985 in Madeira, Portugal. He's 1 meter 85 centimeters tall. He's slim and he has short dark hair and brown eyes.

2 Ronaldo first played soccer when he was three years old, and he turned professional when he was only ten. He played for Sporting in Portugal and then Manchester United. In 2009, he moved to Real Madrid in Spain. He's also on the Portuguese national team.

3 Ronaldo won his first big trophy with Manchester United in 2007, when they were English Premier League champions. He also won the Club World Cup with Manchester United in 2008.

> **○ Glossary**
> trophy = a prize for winning a competition

1 Read the text and answer the questions.

1 Which paragraph is about Ronaldo's career in general, which about the things he won, and which about personal details?
2 Where was he born?
3 How tall is he?
4 Which club did he play for first?
5 When did he win his first big trophy?

2 Study the key phrases. Match the phrases with the three paragraphs in the model text. Then look at the text again and check.

> **KEY PHRASES ○ Sports biography**
>
> 1 His / Her full name is ... .
> 2 He / She turned professional when ... .
> 3 He / She won ... in ... .
> 4 He / She has ... hair and ... eyes.
> 5 He / She was born on ... .
> 6 He / She first ... when he / she was (three) years old.
> 7 He / She also won ... .

Language point: *also*

3 Read the rule and the examples. Then choose the correct position for *also* in sentences 1–4.

> **○ RULE**
>
> *Also* comes after the verb *be* and before other verbs:
> He's **also** on the Portuguese national team.
> He **also** won the Club World Cup.

1 They lost against Barcelona. They **lost also / also lost** against Juventus.
2 He is good at singing. **He's also / He also is** good at dancing.
3 We visited New York. We **also went / went also** to Philadelphia.
4 His old video game was boring. It **also was / was also** very easy.

4 ACTIVATE Follow the steps in the writing guide.

> **Notes: Maria Sharapova**
> **Name:** Maria Yuryevna Sharapova
> **Born:** Nyagan, Russia, April 19, 1987
> **Height:** 1 meter 88 centimeters tall
> **Started tennis:** age 4
> **Professional:** 2001
> **First big trophy:**
> Wimbledon championship 2004

> **○ WRITING GUIDE**
>
> **A TASK**
>
> Write a profile of Maria Sharapova or an athlete of your choice.
>
> **B THINK AND PLAN**
>
> Read the notes about Maria Sharapova. What information do you want to put in each paragraph?
> **Paragraph 1:** name,
> **Paragraph 2:** ___
> **Paragraph 3:** ___
>
> **C WRITE**
>
> Write your profile and follow your paragraph plan. Use the model text and the key phrases.
>
> **D CHECK**
>
> • simple past verbs   • description vocabulary
> • spelling and punctuation

Vocabulary

1 Complete the lists with the words in the box.

> tall bought volleyball beard lose
> bike riding brown race

1 short medium height ___
2 blue green ___
3 glasses mustache ___
4 made sold ___
5 game competition ___
6 win beat ___
7 skiing swimming ___
8 basketball hockey ___

2 Complete the conversation with the words in the box.

> record track and field race dark tall
> team score competitions play

A Who is that ¹___ boy with the ²___ hair?
B That's Tim. He's a very good athlete. He takes part in a lot of ³___. He won the 100 meter ⁴___ last week. He broke the school ⁵___.
A What about you? Are you into ⁶___?
B No, I'm not. But I ⁷___ soccer. I play for the school ⁸___. We were second in the championship last year.
A Second? That's not bad. Did you ⁹___ any goals?
B No, I didn't. I'm the goalkeeper!

Language focus

3 Complete the sentences with the past form of the verbs in parentheses.

1 Tom ___ breakfast early this morning. (eat)
2 He ___ the bus to the mall. (take)
3 He ___ Jim at a café. (meet)
4 They ___ coffee. (have)
5 Jon ___ to a new store. (go)
6 He ___ a new video game. (buy)

4 Write questions and short answers about you in the simple past.

have a big breakfast

> Did you have a big breakfast?   No, I didn't.

1 meet a friend last night
2 go to the mall on Saturday
3 make a pizza last night
4 write an e-mail yesterday
5 have coffee at breakfast
6 see a movie on TV

5 Write questions in the simple past. Then match the questions with answers a–f.

he / meet / his friends / last weekend
Did he meet his friends last weekend? a

1 where / they / go / last night
2 when / she / buy / a computer
3 what / you / have / for dinner
4 they / win / the game / last week
5 you / go / home / early / last night

a No, he didn't.   d Pizza.
b Yes, we did.   e No, they didn't. They lost.
c On Saturday.   f To the movies.

Communication

6 Choose the correct responses to the sentences.

1 Did you have a good weekend?
   a Fine, thanks.   b Why not?   c Not really.
2 I went to a basketball game.
   a Oh dear.   b Was it good?   c OK.
3 I think this is the correct answer.
   a Yes, you're right.   b Yes, I don't agree.
   c It looks like.
4 What did you do on Saturday?
   a I play tennis.   b I go shopping.
   c I watched TV.
5 I think the party is fun.
   a I don't think so.   b I don't think.   c OK.

Listening

7 ⊙ 3.08 Listen to a conversation and complete the sentences.

Harry played ¹___ on Saturday afternoon. His team ²___ the game. In the evening, he went to a ³___.

Kate went ⁴___ on Saturday morning. In the afternoon, she met Tina at the ⁵___. They ⁶___ a DVD in the evening. The movie was very ⁷___. On Sunday, Kate played ⁸___ with her brother.

Rules

1 Choose a trump card and read the first clue to your partner.
2 If your partner guesses the answer, he/she scores 50 points.
3 If your partner doesn't guess the answer, read the second clue.
   Your partner scores 40 points if he/she guesses the answer.
4 Continue until your partner guesses the answer.
   Then listen to your partner's clues.
5 The winner is the person with the highest score.

Who am I?

Clue 1 He's an actor.
       50 points
Clue 2 He was born in California, U.S.
       40 points
Clue 3 He sometimes wears these clothes.
       30 points
Clue 4 His last name starts with G.
       20 points
Clue 5 His first name is Andrew, but his
       nickname is Andy.
       10 points

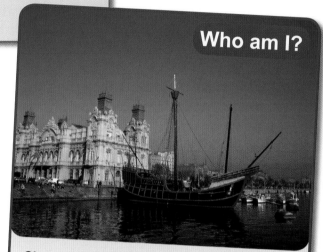

Who am I?

Clue 1 He was an explorer.
       50 points
Clue 2 He was born in Genoa, Italy.
       40 points
Clue 3 This was his famous boat.
       30 points
Clue 4 His last name starts with C.
       20 points
Clue 5 His first name was Christopher.
       10 points

1 Read the rules and play the trump card game with a partner.

2 Make a trump card. Follow the steps in the project checklist.

3 Play the trump card game with five people in your class. Make a note of your score. Who is the winner?

⬤ PROJECT CHECKLIST

1 Think of a famous person, such as a writer, a musician, an explorer, a president, a scientist, an artist, an actor, or an inventor.

2 Find information about the person on the Internet or in a book and write five clues about:

   Clue 1: his or her job
   Clue 2: his or her place of birth
   Clue 3: a famous object or interesting fact about the person
   Clue 4: the first letter of his or her last name
   Clue 5: his or her first name or nickname

3 Find a picture on the Internet or in a magazine, and stick it on a card. Write the clues and points on the card.

4 Write the name of the person on the back of the card.

8

Expedition

Start thinking

1 Where in the world are there jungles?
2 What is the average temperature in Antarctica?
3 What are the mountains from Canada to the U.S. called?

Aims

Communication: I can ...

- talk about what to do on an expedition.
- understand an adventure story.
- talk about plans and intentions.
- talk about the weather.
- make predictions about the future.
- make and respond to suggestions.
- write a blog about an expedition.

Vocabulary

- Travel equipment
- Weather conditions

Language focus

- Imperatives
- *be going to*: affirmative, negative, and questions
- *will* and *won't*
- *so*

Reach Out Options

Extra listening and speaking

The weather forecast

⇨ Page 95

Curriculum extra

Natural science: Weather and climate

⇨ Page 103

Culture

Famous explorers

⇨ Page 111

Vocabulary puzzles

Travel equipment; Weather conditions

⇨ Page 119

VOCABULARY ■ Travel equipment
I can talk about what to do on an expedition.

1 🔊 3.13 Match the equipment with pictures 1–12 on page 79. Then listen and check. Which four things are not in the pictures?

1 tent

> map compass rope backpack satellite phone
> sleeping bag sunglasses sunscreen gloves
> flashlight stove ~~tent~~ insect repellent helmet
> first aid kit waterproof clothes

2 Do the *Rainforest Survival* quiz on page 79. Then check your answers with the key. Do you agree with your result?

Language point: Imperatives

3 Complete the table with imperatives from the quiz. Do we use imperatives for instructions or descriptions?

Affirmative	Negative
Go back.	Don't worry.

> **More practice**
> ⇨ Workbook page 65

4 Complete the sentences with the affirmative or negative imperative form of the verbs in the box.

> swim use forget ~~attack~~ make wear look

Don't attack snakes or other animals.

1 ___ in the river. There are crocodiles.
2 ___ sunscreen every day in summer.
3 ___ your flashlight in the day. You need it to see at night.
4 ___ at the compass and find north.
5 ___ dinner on the stove.
6 ___ waterproof clothes. It's going to rain.

5 🔊 3.14 Listen. Which activity in the box are Amy and Jim going to do? What equipment from exercise 1 are they taking?

> kayaking rock climbing caving trekking
> mountain biking snowboarding paragliding

6 **ACTIVATE** Imagine that you are in the rainforest. Invent dialogues using these words and phrases.

Quickly! Hey! Watch out! Please	pass move touch use help look in etc.	the first aid kit! me with this. the tent! that stove! my flashlight! your sleeping bag! etc.

💬 Quickly! Pass me my flashlight! 💬 Why? What's the matter?

💬 I think there's a snake in my sleeping bag!

Rainforest Survival

1
2
3
4
6
5
11
12
10 **Brazil**
9
8
7

Imagine you're going to go on an expedition to the Amazon. Can you survive in the rainforest? Read the situations and decide what to do.

1 You can't find your map.
  a Go back and look for it.
  b Don't worry. It isn't important in the rainforest.

2 Your compass isn't working.
  a Look at the moon. It's always in the west.
  b Watch the sun. It's always in the west at the end of the day.

3 You don't have any insect repellent.
  a Stay near the river. Mosquitoes don't like water.
  b Wear your waterproof clothes.

4 You see a dangerous snake.
  a Be quiet. Snakes don't usually attack humans.
  b Shine your flashlight at it. Snakes hate bright lights.

5 You're cold in your tent.
  a Light the stove inside your tent to keep warm.
  b Get in your sleeping bag.

6 You're hungry and you see some fruit.
  a Don't eat it. Maybe it's dangerous for humans.
  b Eat a little bit, then wait an hour. Eat more if you're OK.

7 A person in your group can't walk.
  a Use your satellite phone and call for help.
  b Give the person your first aid kit. Then go and get help.

Points

1	a: 2	b: 0
2	a: 0	b: 2
3	a: 0	b: 2
4	a: 2	b: 0
5	a: 0	b: 2
6	a: 2	b: 0
7	a: 2	b: 0

Key
More than 10 points: Well done!
You can survive in a rainforest if necessary.
Between 6 and 8 points: Not bad!
But only go to the rainforest with a group.
Fewer than 4 points: Stay home.
You're going to be safer there.

⬜ *Finished?*
You are taking a group on a desert survival expedition.
Write instructions using imperatives.
Bring a tent and a sleeping bag.
Don't forget ...

My brother Peter and I were on a jungle wildlife vacation with six other people and Diego our guide. It was an amazing experience and we saw lots of monkeys, crocodiles, and huge snakes. But one morning Peter and I did a very stupid thing.

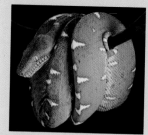

We wanted to take pictures of monkeys. We got up early and walked into the jungle. We didn't have to go far before we heard some monkeys. We were excited and we followed the monkeys for about ten minutes. Suddenly, Peter stopped. He was worried. "I'm not going to walk further," he said. "We'll get lost. I'm going back."

We looked around us. There were trees everywhere. The campsite wasn't far, but we had no idea which direction to take. "I think we are already lost," Peter said. "How are we going to get back? Nobody knows where we are. They'll never find us."

Then it started to rain. Luckily, I had a waterproof coat. We sat on our backpacks with the coat over our heads. There were lots of mosquitoes and we didn't have any insect repellent. We were scared and miserable.

After two hours, we heard a noise. It was Diego and he was angry. "You're very lucky," he said. But we were very happy. "We're never going to follow monkeys again," we promised. Diego laughed, "Come on. Let's go back to camp."

1 Look at the pictures. Where are the people? What are they doing?

2 ● 3.15 Read and listen to Kevin's story and choose the best title a–c. What stupid thing did Kevin and Peter do?
   a Camping in the jungle
   b Lost in the jungle
   c A jungle adventure

3 Read the text again and write *true* or *false*. Correct the false sentences.
   1 Kevin was with six other people in the jungle.
   2 Kevin and Peter went into the jungle early in the morning.
   3 They wanted to explore the jungle.
   4 Everywhere looked the same in the jungle.
   5 They were far from the campsite when they got lost.
   6 They waited for two hours in the rain.

4 BUILD YOUR VOCABULARY Find these adjectives in the text. Which adjectives express positive feelings? When did you last feel like this? Write sentences about your experiences using the adjectives. Then compare with a partner.

   scared   miserable   excited   lucky
   angry   worried

   I was lucky when I found my house keys in the snow.

5 ABOUT YOU Ask and answer the questions.
   1 How often do you sleep in a tent?
   2 Do you like camping? Why / Why not?
   3 When was the last time you were lucky or did something stupid?
   4 Can you remember a time when you were lost? What happened? How did you feel?

LANGUAGE FOCUS ■ *be going to*: affirmative, negative, and questions
I can talk about plans and intentions.

1 Complete the sentences with the words in the box and look at the examples. Then complete the rules.

> 's   aren't   going   'm   to take

I'**m** going to visit the U.S. next year.
You're going ¹___ a tent.
She ²___ going to meet a friend.
We ³___ going to camp.
They're ⁴___ to explore the jungle.

Is she going to stay? Yes, she is. / No, she isn't.
Are you going to stay? Yes, I am. / No, I'm not.
Are we / they going to stay? Yes, we / they are. /
No, we / they aren't.

◯ RULES

1 We use *going to* to talk about **present /
   future** plans and intentions.
2 We make questions with: ***do* / *be*** +
   pronoun / noun + *going to* + verb

(More practice ⟹ Workbook pages 65, 67)

2 Choose the correct words.
   1 My friend **is / are** going to walk into town.
   2 They **aren't / isn't** going to buy anything.
   3 You **isn't / aren't** going to make dinner.
   4 They are going to **having / have** lunch now.
   5 I **aren't / 'm not** going to use the computer.
   6 We're going to **wearing / wear** waterproof
     clothes.

3 Complete the text with the verbs in the box
   and the correct form of *be going to*.

> eat   learn   write   see   not see   read
> ~~walk~~   not travel   not take   meet   call

Explorer Ray Fines is traveling to the U.S. on Saturday
and he **is going to walk** 5,000 kilometers from New York to
Los Angeles. He ¹___ on buses or in cars. He ²___ his family
for ten months, but he ³___ his wife every week. "I'm very
excited about this expedition," says Ray.
"I ⁴___ a lot of things about the U.S. I ⁵___ some fantastic
scenery and I ⁶___ a lot of different people."
Ray ⁷___ and sleep in cheap hotels. He ⁸___ any camping
equipment in his backpack. Ray's friends ⁹___ about his
expedition on the Internet because he ¹⁰___ a blog on his
laptop every night.

4 Write questions about Ray Fines. Then ask and
   answer with a partner.

how / travel   *How is Ray going to travel?*

(How is Ray going to travel?)   (He's going to walk.)

   1 how many kilometers / walk
   2 where / start his trip
   3 where / finish
   4 sleep / in cheap hotels
   5 what / see
   6 who / meet
   7 take / camping equipment
   8 what / write every night

(Pronunciation: Sentence stress and rhythm
  ⟹ Workbook page 92)

5 **ACTIVATE** Find out about your partner's
   future plans. Use the time expressions in A
   and the phrases in B or your own ideas.

A (this evening   tomorrow   on Saturday
     on Sunday   next Monday
     over summer vacation)

B (watch TV   go shopping   meet friends
     do sports   go on a trip   have a party)

(*What are you going to do this evening?*)

(*I'm going to watch TV.*)

(*Are you going to meet friends tomorrow?*)

(*No, I'm not. I'm going to stay at home.*)

◯ *Finished?*
**Imagine the perfect vacation. Write about
your plans.**
*I'm going to take a vacation in Hawaii.
I'm going to stay in a luxury hotel.*

1 🔘 3.16 Match six of the words in the box with the pictures. Then listen and check.

> sunny   cold   foggy   windy   icy   snowy
> hot   rainy   cloudy   stormy

2 Work in pairs. Mime and guess weather words in exercise 1.

> Is it snowy?   No, it isn't.

> Is it windy?   Yes, it is!

STUDY STRATEGY ○ **Nouns from adjectives**

3 Match the nouns with adjectives in exercise 1. Which word doesn't change?

> wind   storm   rain   sun   snow
> cold   heat   cloud   fog   ice

4 🔘 3.17 Look at the picture and listen to an interview with Ken Ford. Choose the correct answer.

Ken Ford is going to study ...
   a penguins in the Antarctic in the summer.
   b polar bears at the South Pole in November.
   c ice in the Antarctic in the summer.

5 🔘 3.17 Listen again and write *true* or *false*. Correct the false sentences.

  1 Ken is going to walk to the South Pole.
  2 He won't see polar bears.
  3 He thinks he will see penguins.
  4 It won't be very cold in November.
  5 It will be very windy there.
  6 He's going to take his cell phone.

6 **ACTIVATE** Work in pairs. Ask and answer questions about the weather. Use the phrases in the box and words in exercises 1 and 3.

> today   yesterday   last weekend
> tomorrow   in winter / summer / fall /
> spring / November

> What's the weather like today?

> It's hot and sunny today.

> What's the weather usually like in November?

> It's usually cold and there's sometimes fog.

LANGUAGE FOCUS ■ *will* and *won't*
I can make predictions about the future.

8

1 Complete the sentences from exercise 5 on page 82. Then answer the questions.

Ken ¹___ walk to the South Pole.
He ²___ see polar bears.
He thinks he ³___ see penguins.
It ⁴___ be very windy there.
He ⁵___ take his cell phone.

1 Which two sentences are plans?
2 Which three sentences are predictions?
3 What is the negative form of *will*?

2 Match the questions with the answers. Then complete the rules.

1 Will he see penguins?
2 Will it be windy?
3 Will polar bears attack him?

a No, they won't.
b Yes, he will.
c Yes, it will.

> **○ RULES**
>
> 1 In questions with *will*, the word order is:
>   ¹___ + noun / pronoun + verb.
> 2 In short answers, the word order is *Yes,* /
>   ²___ + pronoun + *will* / ³___

(More practice ⇨ Workbook page 67)

3 Write sentences with *will* and *won't* and the verbs in parentheses.

We ___ warm clothes. (take)
We'll take warm clothes.

1 I ___ my cell phone. (not use)
2 It ___ cold in the Antarctic. (be)
3 I think she ___ me tonight. (call)
4 You ___ lost because you have a map. (not get)
5 I hope we ___ penguins. (see)
6 It ___ tomorrow, so you won't need waterproof clothes. (not rain)

4 Read situations 1–6 and make sentences with the phrases in parentheses. Use *will* and *won't*.

We have a compass. (get lost)
We won't get lost.

1 He doesn't have a stove. (eat hot food)
2 We have a flashlight. (see in the dark)
3 She has a new sleeping bag. (be cold)
4 They have a satellite phone. (talk to friends)
5 You have sunscreen. (burn in the sun)
6 I don't have waterproof clothes. (get wet)

5 Write questions about the future using the verbs in the box. Then ask and answer with a partner.

> ~~be~~   change   melt   kill   study
> become   live

the weather / cold tonight ✘
Will the weather be cold tonight?   No, it won't.

1 the weather / in the future ✔
2 polar bears / extinct ✔
3 people / in the Arctic ✘
4 scientists / the weather ✔
5 all the Arctic ice / in the next ten years ✘
6 people / all the mosquitoes ✘

6 **ACTIVATE** Write predictions about your future. Use the phrases below and your own ideas. Then ask and answer with people in your class.

> live in a different country   get a job
> visit the Antarctic / the U.S.   have children
> be rich / famous   get married
> go to college   be a scientist

> Will you go to college?
>
> No, I won't. I'll get a job.

> **○ Finished?**
> Write four predictions about the future. Think about: animals, rainforests, people, countries …
> *I think a lot of animals will become extinct.*

Oliver	What's the matter, Diana?
Diana	I think we're lost. I can't find the museum on the map.
Oliver	Oh, no! ¹___
Diana	Why don't we find a taxi?
Oliver	²___
Diana	Well, what do you suggest?
Oliver	³___
Diana	We can't do that. We don't know which bus to take.
Oliver	All right, then. ⁴___
Diana	⁵___ Excuse me!

1 Look at the picture. What are Diana and Oliver looking at? Why?

2 🔊 3.18 **Complete the dialogue with sentences a–e. Then listen and check.**

a That's a good idea!

b I'm not sure about that.

c Let's ask someone.

d How about taking the bus?

e What are we going to do?

3 🔊 3.19 **Listen to the key phrases. Which phrases are for making suggestions and which are for responding? Then practice the dialogue in exercise 1.**

> **KEY PHRASES ◯ Making and responding to suggestions**
>
> Why don't we (find a taxi)?
> I'm not sure about that.
> How about (taking the bus)?
> We can't do that.
> Let's (ask someone).
> That's a good idea!

4 🔊 3.20 **Read the dialogue. Which do you think are the correct suggestions? Listen and complete. Then practice with a partner.**

1 carry Kelly / stay here

2 go to a doctor / find a taxi

3 call her mom / call the school

Elijah	What's the matter?
Sofia	Kelly fell and hurt her leg. She can't walk.
Elijah	What are we going to do?
Sofia	Let's ¹___.
Elijah	We can't do that. It's getting late.
Sofia	How ²___?
Elijah	I'm not sure about that.
Sofia	Why ³___?
Elijah	OK. That's a good idea.

5 **ACTIVATE Look at the situations. Make new mini-dialogues with a partner. Use the dialogue in exercise 4 to help you.**

1 I'm bored.
   study English / watch a DVD / go to bed early

2 It's raining.
   stay at home / go to a café / visit a museum

3 I'm hungry.
   go to a restaurant / buy a sandwich / make a pizza

> I'm bored!   Why don't we watch a DVD?

1 Read the model text and answer the questions.

1 Is the writer at the campsite on August 15?
2 What's the weather like on the first day of the expedition?
3 What day did the writer go kayaking?
4 What happened when he went kayaking?
5 When is the writer going to go walking in the mountains?

2 Study the key phrases. Decide whether each phrase is about the past, the present or the future.

> **KEY PHRASES ○ Writing a blog**
>
> Here I am in my ….
> We're going to stay ….
> We had a … time.
> I'm going to go on a / an … next ….
> This is me in my ….

Language point: *so*

3 Match 1–6 with a–f and write sentences using *so*.

I'm going to take my laptop, so I can continue this blog.
I fell in the water five times, so I know!

1 It's rainy.
2 We don't have a tent.
3 It's interesting.
4 It's hot.
5 We're lost.
6 It's cold.

a I'm going to swim in the river.
b We're going to wear waterproof clothes.
c We're going to get into our sleeping bags.
d We aren't going to go camping.
e I'm going to write a blog about it.
f I'm going to look at the map.

4 **ACTIVATE** Follow the steps in the writing guide.

Saturday, August 15
I'm going to go on a camping trip next Saturday. We're going to stay at a campsite in the Rocky Mountains. I'm going to take my laptop, so I can continue this blog.

Saturday, August 22
Here I am in my tent. It's hot and sunny and we're staying next to a river. I'm going to take lots of pictures because the mountains are spectacular. We're going to go kayaking on the river later.

Sunday, August 23
This is me in my kayak. We had a fantastic time, but the river was really cold. I fell in the water five times, so I know! We're going to walk in the mountains tomorrow. I'm going to take my compass … and a first aid kit!

> **○ WRITING GUIDE**
>
> **A TASK**
>
> Write a blog about a trip or adventure.
>
> **B THINK AND PLAN**
>
> **Day 1**
> Think of the details of your trip:
> Where? (e.g. hiking in the Andes, mountain biking in the Rocky Mountains) When?
> What equipment are you going to take?
> **Day 2**
> Describe the weather and the place.
> What activities are you going to do later?
> (e.g. caving, rock climbing, trekking, mountain biking, etc.)
> **Day 3**
> What were the activities like?
> What are you going to do tomorrow?
>
> **C WRITE**
>
> Write your blog. Follow the model text and use the key phrases.
>
> **D CHECK**
>
> • sentences with *so*
> • spelling and punctuation

Vocabulary

1 Match the words in the box with the definitions.

> gloves   stove   insect repellent   compass
> sunscreen   sunglasses   backpack
> flashlight

1 You carry it on your back.
2 You use it to see in the dark.
3 You need it in hot and sunny weather.
4 You wear them on your hands.
5 You wear them when it's sunny.
6 Mosquitoes don't bite you when you use it.
7 You cook food on it.
8 It shows you the direction.

2 Write the adjective form of these nouns.

> wind   sun   fog   snow   cloud   storm
> ice   rain   heat   cold

wind – windy

Language focus

3 Write affirmative and negative sentences using the correct form of *be going to*.

(not hunt animals / take pictures)
I'm not going to hunt animals. I'm going to take pictures.
1 Emma (not take a tent / sleep outside)
2 the students (not study / explore the rainforest)
3 he (not travel by boat / fly)
4 we (not ask someone / look at the map)
5 you (not catch the frogs / count them)
6 they (not have any hot water / wash in the river)

4 Write questions using *be going to*. Then match the questions with the answers a–h.

How are they going to travel?   **g**
1 what equipment / Lucy / take
2 be hot / there
3 you / take pictures
4 what / you / do there
5 what / they / see
6 what / Tim / wear
7 they / go by train

a Yes, I am.
b Waterproof clothes.
c A map and a camera.
d Yes, it is.
e I'm going to take pictures of animals.
f No, they aren't.
g In a canoe.
h Polar bears.

5 Order the words to make questions with *will*. Then write short answers.

be / the weather / tomorrow / will / cold ✗
Will the weather be cold tomorrow?   **No, it won't.**
1 a / scientists / will / new species / find ✔
2 see / monkeys / you / in the jungle / will ✔
3 it / next winter / a lot / will / snow ✗
4 arrive / we / early / will ✔
5 need / waterproof clothes / you / will ✗
6 win / will / the game / they ✗

Communication

6 Complete the mini-dialogues with the words in the box.

> don't   about   Let's   matter   like

1 A What's the weather ___ today?
  B It's hot and sunny.
2 A I'm really tired.
  B Why ___ you go to bed early tonight?
3 A What's the ___?
  B I'm bored.
4 A It's raining.
  B ___ watch a DVD.
5 A How ___ going to a restaurant?
  B We can't do that.

Listening

7 🔊 3.21 Listen and choose the correct words.

Anna is going to travel to the ¹**Arctic / Antarctic**. Anna is ²**an explorer / a scientist**. She's going to study the ³**weather / ice** there. She's going to go in ⁴**June / July** because it'll be summer then. It will be sunny, but it will also be pretty ⁵**cold / windy**. The North Pole is ⁶**warmer / colder** than the South Pole. The average temperature in summer is about ⁷**0° / 10°** Celsius. She's going to take a ⁸**cell / satellite** phone, so she can talk to her family.

Listening

1 Look at the pictures. Where are the people? What are they doing?

2 ⬤ 3.22 Listen to a conversation. Where are the friends going to camp?

3 ⬤ 3.22 Listen again and complete the sentences.

1 The weather will be ___ on the weekend.
2 Tim went camping in the mountains last ___.
3 Lucy is going ___ in the ocean.
4 They are going to cook some ___.
5 Lucy has a tent and a small ___.
6 Lucy is going to make some ___.
7 They are going to travel by ___.
8 Jon is going to take a ___, a ___, and a ___.

Speaking

4 Work in groups of three and prepare a conversation. Imagine you are planning a camping weekend. Answer these questions.

1 Where are you going to go?
2 What are you going to do there?
3 What is the weather forecast?
4 How are you going to travel?
5 What will you take?

5 Have a conversation. Use your ideas in exercise 4 and the chart below to help you. One of you is A, one of you is B and one of you is C. When you have finished, change roles.

A *Why don't we [activity]?*

B Reply and ask where.

A Suggest a place.

B *I'm not sure about that.* Give a reason.

A Suggest another place.

B Agree and ask about transportation.

A Reply.

B *What are we going to take?*

A *We'll need ... . I have ... .*

B *I can bring .... What's the weather forecast?*

A Reply.

B *Let's call ....*

A *Hi. It's ... .* Give details of your plans. *Do you want to come?*

C Reply and ask about equipment.

A Reply.

C *I have ....*

Writing

6 Write a description of a terrible weekend. Imagine you went camping last weekend and a lot of things went wrong. You can use the situation in the listening or in exercise 4. Think about the following ideas and say what happened and how you felt.

> transportation   the weather   activities
> food   equipment

Begin like this:
Last weekend, I went camping with ... and ... .
It was terrible! We met on Saturday morning at ...
We traveled to ...

EXTRA LISTENING AND SPEAKING ■ Identifying people

I can talk about people in a picture.

1 Look at picture A. Where is this picture from?
a a photo album
b a cell phone
c a website

2 🔘 1.15 Study the key phrases. Listen to the conversation and match the names with 1–3 in picture A. Who is not in the picture?

Jan   Dan   Maria   Lucas   Emma

> **KEY PHRASES ⬤ Talking about a picture**
>
> in the middle   on the right   in the back
> on the left   next to

3 🔘 1.15 Listen again and answer the questions.

1 What's Dan's website about?
2 What is Lucas good at?
3 What does Maria like?
4 What does Jan have?

4 🔘 1.16 Look at picture B. Listen and repeat the dialogue.

Emma Hey, Dan. Look at this picture of me and my friends.
Dan Who's that in the middle?
Emma That's my friend, Chen. He's very good at sports.
Dan And who's that next to Chen?
Emma That's Tim. He has a cool hat.

5 ACTIVATE Look at picture C and think of names and interests for the people. Then ask and answer questions using the key phrases.

Who's that in the back?

That's Tom. He's into music.

EXTRA LISTENING AND SPEAKING ■ Giving personal information

I can understand and give personal information.

1 Match the personal information with the words in the box.

> e-mail address   name   zip code
> phone number

1 Mark Ward
2 80101
3 303-555-1276
4 mark@mymail.com

2 🔘 1.29 Listen to a phone conversation. Where's the receptionist?

> a shopping mall   an Internet café
> a community center   a library

3 🔘 1.29 Study the key phrases. Then listen to the conversation again. Complete the missing information.

> **KEY PHRASES ◯ Giving information**
>
> 0 = zero
> @ = at
> . = dot

Name
Julia ¹___

Zip code
²___ 14

Home phone number
³___-555-6432

Cell phone number
212-555-⁴___

E-mail address
⁵___ @mymail.com

4 🔘 1.30 Listen and write the phone numbers you hear. Then listen and repeat.

5 🔘 1.31 Listen and repeat the dialogue.

Receptionist	What's your name?
Mark	Mark Ward.
Receptionist	What's your zip code?
Mark	80101.
Receptionist	And your phone number?
Mark	It's 303-555-1276.
Receptionist	What's your e-mail address?
Mark	It's mark@mymail.com.

6 ACTIVATE Change the words in blue in exercise 5 and practice a dialogue about Susan Tanner. Then change roles and practice a new dialogue using your personal information.

> Susan Tanner
> susantanner44@bigpost.net
> 33156
> 305-555-1386

EXTRA LISTENING AND SPEAKING ■ Talking about schedules

I can tell the time and say when I do things.

3

1 Match the clocks with the times in the box.

> three o'clock   five past seven   quarter past nine   twenty-five past two
> half past six   ten to two   twenty to twelve   quarter to eleven

2 🔘 1.41 **Listen and write the times you hear. Then listen and repeat.**

1 10:20

3 🔘 1.42 **Listen to a phone conversation. How many sports does Matt ask about?**

4 🔘 1.42 **Study the key phrases. Then listen to the conversation again and complete the schedule.**

> **KEY PHRASES ☐ Talking about schedules**
>
> What time does the swimming pool open / close?
> What time does it start / finish?
> At eight o'clock.
> From five o'clock to quarter past six on Mondays.

5 🔘 1.43 **Look at the schedule. Listen and repeat the dialogue.**

David	What time is the swimming pool open on Wednesday?
Receptionist	It's open from quarter to ten to eight o'clock.
David	When's basketball?
Receptionist	It's on Tuesday at quarter to four.
David	What time does it finish?
Receptionist	It finishes at quarter past five.

6 ACTIVATE **Change the words in blue in exercise 5 using information in the schedule. Then practice your new dialogue with a partner.**

	MONDAY	TUESDAY	WEDNESDAY
Swimming pool	9:45 a.m. – 8:00 p.m.	10:30 a.m. – ¹_____	9:45 a.m. – 8:00 p.m.
Taekwondo			²_____ – 6:00 p.m.
³_____	4:45 p.m. –	⁴_____	
Basketball		3:45 p.m. – 5:15 p.m.	

EXTRA LISTENING AND SPEAKING ■ Talking about future arrangements

I can talk about my plans.

1 Study the key phrases. Then say dates 1–6.

> **KEY PHRASES ○ Saying dates**
>
> July 31 = July thirty-first
> May 22 = May twenty-second
> February 23 = February twenty-third
> April 5 = April fifth

1 June 1
2 October 14
3 December 3
4 August 30
5 January 2
6 September 9

2 🔘 2.12 Listen and write the dates you hear. Then listen and repeat.

3 🔘 2.13 Listen to a conversation. Where are Steve and David going?

4 🔘 2.13 Listen to the conversation again and complete the website.

5 🔘 2.14 Listen and repeat the dialogue.

Ruby There's a concert at The Ice Club on November 6. I'm going with Sally. Do you want to come?

Paul No, sorry, I'm busy. I'm staying with my grandparents that weekend. It's my grandpa's 80th birthday on November 3. We're having a party.

Ruby That's too bad.

6 ACTIVATE Change the words in blue in exercise 5 using your own ideas. Then practice your new dialogue with a partner.

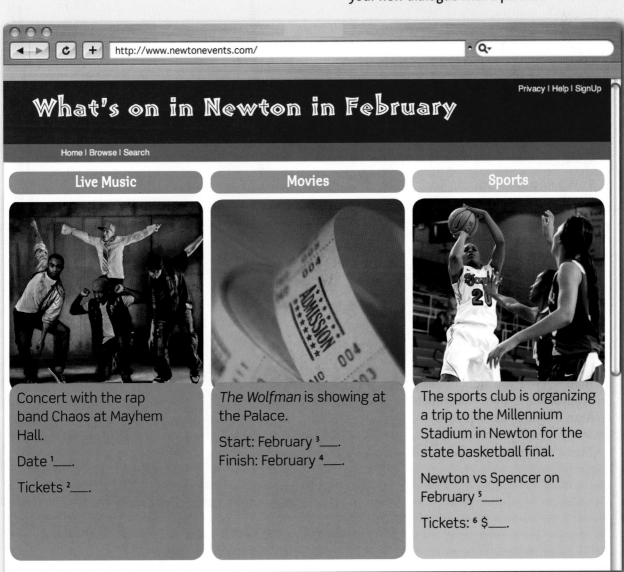

http://www.newtonevents.com/

Privacy I Help I SignUp

What's on in Newton in February

Home I Browse I Search

Live Music

Concert with the rap band Chaos at Mayhem Hall.

Date ¹___.

Tickets ²___.

Movies

The Wolfman is showing at the Palace.

Start: February ³___.
Finish: February ⁴___.

Sports

The sports club is organizing a trip to the Millennium Stadium in Newton for the state basketball final.

Newton vs Spencer on February ⁵___.

Tickets: ⁶ $___.

Reach Out Options

EXTRA LISTENING AND SPEAKING ■ Ordering food
I can order food and drink.

5

1 Study the key phrases. Then say prices 1–6.

> **KEY PHRASES ○ Saying prices**
>
> 50¢ = fifty cents
> $3.00 = three dollars
> $1.40 = one dollar and forty cents
> $3.09 = three dollars and nine cents

1 $4.50
2 70¢
3 $2.80
4 $7.20
5 46¢
6 $6.07

2 ◉ 2.27 Listen and write the prices you hear. Then listen and repeat.

3 ◉ 2.28 Listen to the conversation and write Susan or Joey.

cheeseburger **Joey**
French fries [1]___
ham sandwich [2]___
chocolate ice cream [3]___
soda [4]___
apple juice [5]___

4 ◉ 2.28 Listen again and answer the questions.

1 What food does Susan like?
2 What is Joey's favorite food on the menu?
3 How much is the ice cream?
4 How much do they pay?

5 ◉ 2.29 Listen and repeat the dialogue.

Man Hello. Can I help you?
Jenny Yes. Can I have pasta and salad, please?
Man Yes, of course. Do you want a drink?
Jenny A soda, please.
Man Here you are. Anything else?
Jenny No, thanks. How much is that?
Man That's $8.10, please.
Jenny Here you are.
Man Thanks.

6 ACTIVATE Study the key phrases below. Then change the words in blue in exercise 5 using information on the menu and practice your new dialogue with a partner.

> **KEY PHRASES ○ Ordering food**
>
> Can I help you?   Can I have ..., please?
> Do you want ...?   Anything else?
> How much is that?   That's ..., please.

MENU

** Special **
Chicken and rice $5.50

Sandwiches
Ham $2.85
Cheese $2.55

Fruit
Pears $1
Bananas $1

Drinks
Milk $1.25
Apple juice $1.25
Soda $1.50

EXTRA LISTENING AND SPEAKING ● Talking about a movie or TV program   **6**

I can talk about a movie or a TV program.

1 Match posters 1–5 with the types of movies in the box.

> comedy   adventure   horror   fantasy   love

2 🔊 2.42 Listen to three dialogues and guess the types of movies.

3 🔊 2.43 Listen to a conversation. What type of movie did Carla watch last night?

4 🔊 2.43 Study the key phrases. Then listen to the conversation again and answer the questions.

> **KEY PHRASES** ◯ **Talking about movies**
>
> Did you do anything interesting?
> What was it called?
> Was it good?
> How about you?
> We watched a (DVD).

1 Why didn't Carla sleep?
2 What time did Beth's parents arrive home?
3 Why were her parents surprised?
4 What did Tom do last night?
5 What are Carla's favorite movies?

5 🔊 2.44 Listen and repeat the dialogue.

Alex Did you do anything interesting last night?
Lisa No, I watched a movie on TV.
Alex What was it called?
Lisa *Ocean Paradise*. It's an adventure story.
Alex Was it good?
Lisa It was pretty exciting. How about you? Did you go out?
Alex No, I watched a TV program about Ancient Greece.
Lisa That sounds boring.
Alex It was!

6 ACTIVATE Change the words in blue in exercise 5 using your own ideas. Then practice your new dialogue with a partner.

EXTRA LISTENING AND SPEAKING ● Talking about video games

I can talk about video games I have played.

1 Match the games with the categories in the box.

driving and racing   simulation   action and adventure   soccer

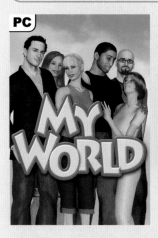
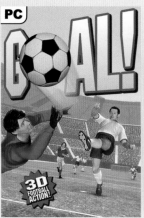

2 🔊 3.09 **Study the key phrases. Then listen to the conversation and complete the table.**

> **KEY PHRASES ◯ Talking about video games**
>
> What did you think of it?
> What's your score for it?
> 8/10 = eight out of ten
> It was fun / great / exciting.
> It was boring / complicated / terrible.

	Ellie's game	Tom's game	Anna's game
Title	*My World*	³ __	⁵ __
Score	¹ __	8/10	⁶ __
Opinion	² __	⁴ __	terrible

3 🔊 3.09 **Listen again. Choose the correct words.**

1 In Ellie's game, the players are **helpers** / **designers**.
2 Ellie was bored after one **hour** / **day**.
3 You **create** / **drive** cars in Tom's game.
4 Tom's game has very **good** / **bad** graphics.
5 In Anna's game, the **characters** / **rules** are complicated.

4 🔊 3.10 **Listen and repeat the dialogue.**

Tim   Which game did you play?
Lisa I played *Goal!*. It's a soccer game.
Tim   What did you think of it?
Lisa It was great. You play soccer for a top team.
Tim   What's your score for it?
Lisa Nine out of ten.

5 ACTIVATE **Change the words in blue in exercise 4 using your own ideas. Then practice your new dialogue with a partner.**

EXTRA LISTENING AND SPEAKING ■ The weather forecast　⑧

I can say what the weather is going to be like next weekend.

1 Match symbols 1–5 with the words in the box.

temperature　rain　sun　wind　cloud

① ② **18** ③ **26** ④ ⑤

2 🔊 3.23 Study the key phrases. Then listen to the weather forecast and complete the table with the information.

> **KEY PHRASES 〇 Talking about the weather**
>
> What's the weather going to be like?
> in the north / south / east / west
> on the north coast
> twenty-two degrees Celsius (22°C)

	San Francisco	Los Angeles	San Diego
Type of weather	¹ __	³ __	⁵ __
Temperature	² __	⁴ __	⁶ __

3 🔊 3.23 Listen again and answer the questions.

1 What's the weather like today?
2 What day of the week is the weather forecast for?
3 What's the weather going to be like in Sacramento?
4 What is the usual weather for summer in California?

4 🔊 3.24 Listen and repeat the dialogue.

Helen I'm going to be in San Diego for the weekend. What's the weather going to be like?
Ben I think it's going to be sunny.
Helen What about the temperature?
Ben It's going to be about 35° Celsius.
Helen Is it going to be windy?
Ben Yes, it is.

5 ACTIVATE Look at the map. Change the words in blue in exercise 4 using information on the map. Practice your new dialogue with a partner.

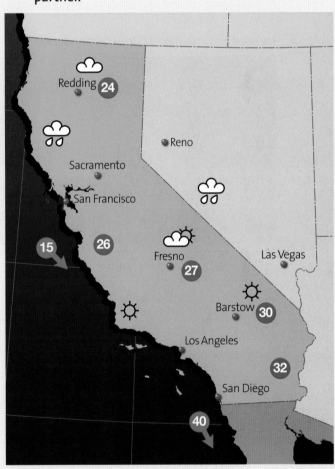

CURRICULUM EXTRA ◼ Visual arts: Color
I can describe the use of color in a picture.

1 Match the words with colors 1–6 on the color wheel.

> blue   orange   green   purple   red   yellow

2 🔊 1.17   Check the meaning of the words. Then listen and complete the sentences.

> secondary   warm   complementary
> ~~primary~~   contrast   cool

1 Red, yellow, and blue are **primary** colors.
2 Orange, green, and purple are ___ colors.
3 Red, orange, and yellow are ___ colors.
4 Green, blue, and purple are ___ colors.
5 Red and green, orange and blue, and yellow and purple are ___ colors.
6 Two complementary colors next to each other create a ___.

3 Look at pictures A and B and complete the texts with the words in the boxes.

> cool   green   contrast

The colors in picture A are ¹___.
There is a lot of blue, ²___, and purple.
There is some yellow, too. There is a ³___ between the yellow and the other colors.

> complementary   warm   blue

There are ⁴___ and cool colors in this picture. There is a contrast between the ⁵___ sky and the orange wheat field. These colors are ⁶___ colors.

4 Look at picture C and answer the questions. Then write a description of the painting using the texts in exercise 3 to help you.

1 What colors are there in the painting?
2 Are the colors warm or cool?
3 Is there a contrast in the painting?
4 Are there complementary colors in the painting?

5 ACTIVATE Choose a picture you like and answer the questions in exercise 4. Write a description of the picture.

CURRICULUM EXTRA ■ Geography: Reading a map

I can ask and answer questions about a map.

1 🔊 1.32 Check the meaning of the words and match them with symbols 1–6. Read and listen to the text and check your answers.

> path   hill   railroad   forest   river   road

| 1 | 2 | 3 | 4 | 5 | 6 |

2 Read the text again. What other symbols are on a map?

MAPS

A map is a representation of a place. It has a scale and a legend. A scale of 1:100,000 means that one centimeter on the map equals 100,000 centimeters, or one kilometer, in the place.

There are some symbols in the legend. An area with green trees is a forest, and a blue line is a river. A black dotted line is a path. There is a small black triangle and a number for a hill. The number, for example 279, means that the hill is 279 meters high. Red lines are roads, and a railroad is a black line with smaller lines on it. A black circle on a railroad is a train station. A red area is a city or town. Next to the red area is the name of the city.

3 Look at map A and choose the correct words.

The scale is ¹**1:100,000 / 1:50,000**. There are a lot of ²**paths / railroads** on this map, and there's one ³**hill / forest**. It is ⁴**246 / 156** meters high. There's also a big ⁵**town / road** and a ⁶**train station / city** on the map.

4 Look at map B and answer the questions.

1 What is the scale of the map?
2 How many hills are there on this map?
3 How high are they?
4 How many forests are there?
5 Are there any roads on the map?
6 Is there a railroad?
7 Are there any paths on the map?
8 Is there a city on the map? What's it called?

5 **ACTIVATE** Work in pairs and draw a map of a place you know or an imaginary place. Then work with another pair and ask and answer the questions in exercise 4 about your maps.

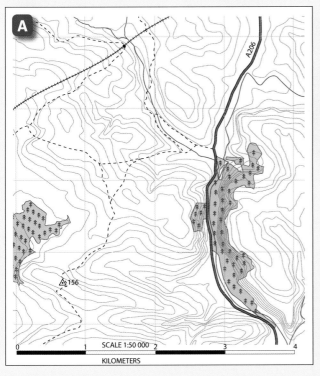

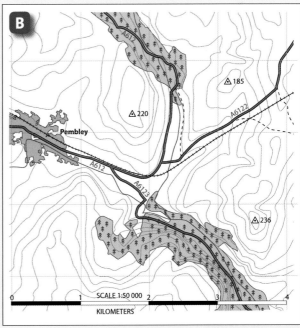

CURRICULUM EXTRA ● Language and literature: Non-verbal language

I can understand a text about different ways to communicate.

3

1 Check the meaning of the words in the box and match them with faces 1–5.

> happy   tired   confused   angry   surprised

2 🔘 1.44 Read and listen to the text. What is non-verbal language? Is it important?

How do people communicate?

Imagine you are in a café in China, but you don't speak Mandarin. A Chinese woman asks you a question and you say, "Sorry, I don't understand." She doesn't speak your language, but she understands you. That's because you look confused. The woman understands your non-verbal language.

In writing, we also use non-verbal language. Colors communicate important information. Everybody understands that red means "stop" or "dangerous". Green means "go" or "safe". We also use pictures and symbols. In this book, a CD symbol means "listen to the audio track".

When we speak, we use words, but we also use non-verbal language. We communicate only 7 percent of the message with words or verbal language. Non-verbal language doesn't use words. In a conversation, we listen to people, but we also watch them. We understand when people are happy, sad, confused, or angry. We use facial expressions and gestures.

People from different countries use different verbal languages to communicate, but everybody understands non-verbal language.

3 Read the text again and write *true* or *false*. Correct the false sentences.

1 Most communication is non-verbal.
2 Verbal language is language with facial expressions.
3 People use gestures in conversation.
4 It's impossible to understand people if we don't speak their language.
5 Red and green communicate the same information everywhere.

4 ACTIVATE Use non-verbal language to communicate these messages to your partner.

> You are disappointed.   You are scared.
> You don't have a pen.   You are cold.
> You don't understand a question.
> It's late.

CURRICULUM EXTRA ■ Natural science: Animals
I can talk about the different animal groups.

④

1 Check the meaning of the words in the box and complete the text with five of the words.

> feathers scales legs hair wings
> lungs fins ~~backbones~~ gills

2 🔘 2.15 **Read and listen to the text. Check your answers in exercise 1. Then answer the questions.**

1 Which type of animal doesn't live on land?
2 Which types of animal have scales?
3 Which type of animal has hair?
4 How are snakes different from other reptiles?
5 Which type of animal is different when it's older?
6 Which type of animal feeds its babies milk?

3 Which group are these animals from? Use the chart to classify them.

> chameleon shark bear owl

1 Does it feed its babies milk?
Yes. It's a mammal. No. Go to number 2.

2 Does it have feathers and wings?
Yes. It's a bird. No. Go to number 3.

3 Does it have fins?
Yes. It's a fish. No. Go to number 4.

4 Does it have scales?
Yes. It's a reptile. No. It's an amphibian.

4 **ACTIVATE** Think of an animal. Ask and answer the questions in exercise 3 and your own questions with a partner. Guess the animal.

Vertebrates

Vertebrates are animals with **backbones**. The following groups are the different types of vertebrate.

Fish

Fish are cold-blooded animals and they live in water. They have scales and ¹___. They don't have lungs. They have gills instead. Most fish lay eggs and they don't look after their babies.

Mammals

All mammals are warm-blooded and they feed their babies milk. Most mammals live on land, for example humans and dogs. Some mammals, like whales, live in water, but they don't have gills. They all have ²___. Most of them have hair and four legs.

Birds

Birds live on land, but some of them look for food in water. They have ³___, two legs, and two wings. Some birds, like ostriches and kiwis, can't fly. All birds lay eggs and they feed their young.

Amphibians

When amphibians are young, they live in water and they don't have lungs. When they are adult, they have lungs and four ⁴___, for example frogs and toads. They lay their eggs in water, but they don't live in water all the time.

Reptiles

Most reptiles live on land. They have lungs and scales, but not gills. They don't have any wings or feathers, and they don't have fins or ⁵___. All the animals in this group, for example chameleons and lizards, have four legs, except for snakes. They are cold-blooded animals and many of them live in warm places.

CURRICULUM EXTRA ◼ Physical education: Rules of a game

I can explain the rules of a team sport.

5

1 Match the verbs in the box with actions 1–7.

catch   pass   bounce   kick   shoot   score   throw

2 🔘 2.30 Read and listen to the text. How many players are there on the court in a basketball game?

A basketball game

Basketball is from the U.S. and all schools in the U.S. have a basketball team. It's also popular in other parts of the world today and many schools have basketball teams for both girls and boys.

Object of the game

In a basketball game, two teams play on a court. There are two baskets, one at each end of the court. There are five players on a team and there are six extra players called substitutes. These players change with the others during the game. The object of the game is for the players to shoot the ball into the basket. The team scores points when the ball goes in the basket. At the end of the game, the team with more points is the winner.

Rules

Basketball is a very fast game and there are a lot of rules to learn. A professional game in the U.S. lasts forty-eight minutes with a fifteen-minute break in the middle. You can run and bounce the ball, or pass the ball to a player on your team. You can only use one hand to bounce the ball and you can't bounce the ball, catch it, and then bounce it again. It's forbidden to kick the ball or to throw it out of the court. You can jump when you shoot the ball into the basket. If you break any of these rules, the other team gets the ball.

3 Read the text again and answer the questions.

1 Where is basketball from?
2 What do the substitutes do?
3 How long is a basketball game?
4 How many hands can you use to bounce a ball?
5 Can you kick the ball?
6 What happens when a player breaks a rule?

4 ACTIVATE Choose a different sport from the box and write three rules. Use the verbs in exercise 1. Your partner guesses the sport.

soccer   volleyball   handball   footvolley

CURRICULUM EXTRA ● Language and literature: Myths and legends

I can talk about myths and legends.

1 Match the words in the box with pictures 1–5.

> god   mountain   goddess   thunder and lightning   war

2 ● 2.45 Read and listen to the text. Which days of the week are missing?

3 Read the text again. Choose the correct words.

1 Norse people lived in the **north** / **south** of Europe.
2 Tyr is the god of **war** / **love**.
3 Thor was Woden's **father** / **son**.
4 Thor was the god of **thunder** / **war**.
5 Frigg was a **god** / **goddess**.

4 Look at the pictures below. The Norse people used them for the other days of the week. Write the correct days.

1 ___day   2 ___day   3 ___day

5 **ACTIVATE** Work in pairs. Write about a character from a popular myth or legend in your country. Use the questions below to help you. Then ask and answer questions with another pair and guess the character.

1 Where and when did the character live?
2 Who was he / she? (a god / goddess, a king / queen, etc.)
3 Was the character a good or a bad person?
4 What was he / she like?
5 Do people use the name of the character for a thing or a place?

Norse gods & goddesses

The Norse people lived in the north of Europe a long time ago. They had many stories about gods and goddesses. We use the names of some of these gods and goddesses for the days of the week in English.

Tyr

The Norse god Tyr was the god of war and he lived on a high mountain. His name became Tuesday.

Woden

Wednesday is "Woden's Day". Woden was the father and ruler of all the gods. Woden was more important than all the other gods.

Thor

Thor was the god of thunder and he was very big and strong. The Norse people used his name for Thursday. It means "Thor's day". Thor lived with his wife and children. There are many stories about Thor's life.

Frigg

Friday comes from "Frigg's Day". Frigg wasn't a god. She was an important goddess, and she was very pretty. Everyone loved her. In some languages, her name means "wife" or "love".

CURRICULUM EXTRA ■ Technology: The Internet
I can understand a text about the history of the Internet.

7

1 Read the introduction of the text. Which of the things in blue do you do on the Internet?

2 3.11 Read and listen to the text. What invention was very important for the development of the Internet?

3 Read the text again and answer the questions.
1 What was the first name for the Internet?
2 Who used the Internet in the early days?
3 What did Ray Tomlinson do?
4 Why did Tim Berners-Lee use the symbol "ch" in his website address?
5 Why did universities create search engines?

4 ACTIVATE Do a survey about how people use the Internet. Ask four students about the things in blue in the text. Then write four sentences using the phrases in the box.

> All four people ...   Two / Three people ...
> One person ...   Nobody ...

All four people write e-mails. Two people buy music.
Nobody downloads e-books.

http://www.theinternet.com/

The Internet

Where do you look for information, play games, watch videos, download e-books, and buy music? What do you use to write e-mails or chat to friends on websites like Facebook or MySpace? More than 1.5 billion people do these things on the Internet every day. Today, the Internet is all over the world, but fifty years ago it did not exist.

The Internet started in 1969 in the U.S. It was called ARPANET at first, but its name soon changed to "the Internet". Universities used it to communicate ideas and information. In those days, computers were enormous machines and not many people used them.

This began to change in 1971 when Ray Tomlinson, an American engineer, sent the first e-mail message. He chose the symbol @ on his keyboard to identify his e-mail address.

The Internet didn't become really popular until Tim Berners-Lee, an English scientist, invented the World Wide Web in 1989.

His invention was very important because it became possible to do a lot more things on the Internet like listening to music and watching videos. He created the first website and named it info.cern.ch. He used the symbol "ch" for Switzerland because he worked in Geneva.

After that, people created millions of websites on every topic. At first, it wasn't easy to find information, so in the early 1990s many universities developed search engines. Lycos was one of the first of these and later, Yahoo! and Google became very popular.

Today, you don't need a big computer to go on the Internet. You can use a smart phone or a tablet with a wi-fi connection. Internet technology is changing all the time and it is changing our lives.

The water cycle

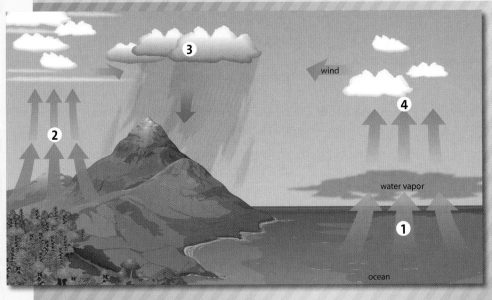

When it's ¹**cloudy / sunny**, the water in rivers and oceans becomes warmer. Some of the water becomes ²**water vapor / rain**, and it goes into the air. This process is called evaporation.

Water from plants and trees also goes into the ³**ocean / air**. This process is called transpiration.

When the water vapor travels higher, it becomes ⁴**colder / warmer**. The water vapor becomes water again, and this makes ⁵**clouds / ice**. This process is called condensation.

⁶**Fog / Wind** moves the clouds over the land and it starts to rain. When it's very cold, it snows. The rain or snow is called precipitation. This water goes into rivers and oceans, and then the water cycle starts again.

1   ● 3.25   Read the text and choose the correct words. Then listen and check your answers.

2   Read the text again and match the words in the box with labels 1–4 in the picture.

> evaporation   transpiration   precipitation   condensation

3   Look at the weather charts for the average precipitation and temperature in Yellowknife and read the text. Find three mistakes in the text.

> Yellowknife is in the north of Canada. It's on the Yellowknife River and it's about 400 kilometers south of the Arctic. It isn't a rainy city, but it's very cold and snowy in the summer (June–August). There's more precipitation in the winter (December–February) than in the summer. It's colder in December than in any other month of the year.

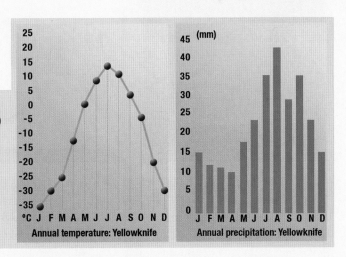

Annual temperature: Yellowknife

Annual precipitation: Yellowknife

4   **ACTIVATE** Look at the information about the average precipitation and temperature in Oxford, England. Draw two weather charts like the ones in exercise 3 to show the information.

	Jan	Feb	Mar	Apr	May	June	July	Aug	Sep	Oct	Nov	Dec
precipitation (mm)	52.3	41.0	41.7	43.3	51.5	54.5	61.1	59.3	60.9	65.5	62.0	55.4
temperature (°C)	3.7	4.2	5.8	8.4	11.7	14.9	16.6	16.2	13.8	10.1	6.4	4.4

CULTURE ▪ Young people around the world

I can write about my favorite sports and interests.

1 🔴 1.18 Look at the pictures and guess what the people's interests are. Who would you like for a friend? Then read and listen to the text. Check your answers.

2 Read the texts again and answer the questions.
1 What sports is Zak into?
2 What is the TV program *Top Gear* about?
3 Where are Daniel's parents from?
4 Who is Thabo Sefolosha?
5 Where is Carla's home?
6 What type of music is she into?

3 YOUR CULTURE Answer the questions.
1 Where are you and your parents from?
2 What are popular sports in your country?
3 What are your and your friends' favorite TV programs?
4 What music is popular with young people in your country?

4 TASK Write a text for the *Friends worldwide* website.
• Write your text on a sheet of paper, but don't write your name. Use the texts below as models.
• Fold your paper and put it with all the other students' texts.
• Take another student's text. Read the text and guess the name of the student.

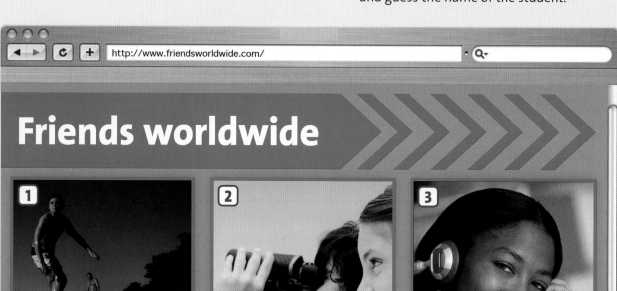

http://www.friendsworldwide.com/

Friends worldwide

A G'day! I'm Zak and I'm from Sydney in Australia. I'm crazy about surfing and the beaches here are fantastic for it. I like rugby and I'm on the school team, but I'm not very good. I'm also interested in computer games and I love cars. My favorite program is *Top Gear*. My sister Jess can't stand it because she hates cars!

B Hi! My name's Daniel and Laura is my sister. Our parents are from Argentina, but we're now in Oklahoma, U.S. We're into basketball and we're fans of the Oklahoma City Thunder. Our favorite player is Thabo Sefolosha. He's from Switzerland. I'm interested in birdwatching and I have some amazing pictures of eagles.

C Hi! I'm Carla Oke and I'm from Manchester in the U.K., but my mom is from Nigeria. I'm really into music. I like hip-hop and my favorite singer is Ms. Dynamite. All my friends love her music, too. I'm not good at sports, but I like soccer on TV. And guess what? I'm a Manchester United fan like all my friends!

CULTURE ■ The United States

I can write a description of a town or city.

1 🔘 1.33 **Look at the map of the United States and match the words in the box with 1–5. Then read and listen to the text. Check your answers.**

New York City   Dallas   Nashville
Los Angeles   Washington

NEW YORK
5
4
DISTRICT OF COLUMBIA
CALIFORNIA
1
3
TENNESSEE
2
TEXAS

I love Nashville

Hi. I'm Anna and I'm from Nashville, in the north of the state of Tennessee. It's a big city, but it's really friendly. There are lots of interesting things to see and do here. Nashville is on the Cumberland River and my favorite place is downtown Nashville. There are bars, restaurants, stores, art galleries, and museums. There is a lot of music there, too. The Country Music Hall of Fame is a fantastic place to visit if you're into music. There's also The Grand Ole Opry, a place where you can hear some of the best country music singers in the world.

My family is American, but we're from different places. My mom's from Dallas, Texas, and my dad's from Los Angeles, California. My sister is at college in the capital city of the U.S., Washington, D.C. That means I have family all over the United States. My favorite city is New York. It's the biggest city in the U.S. There are over eight million people there. It's an exciting place to visit, but the people in Nashville are friendlier!

2 **Read the text again and answer the questions.**

1 Where's Nashville?
2 What is there in downtown Nashville?
3 What is there in Nashville for music fans?
4 What city is Anna's mom from?
5 Where is her sister's college?
6 What is Anna's favorite city?

3 **YOUR CULTURE** **Answer the questions.**

1 What is the capital city of your country? How many people are there in the city?
2 What big cities are in your area?

3 Is your city on a river? What's the name of the river?
4 What is there for tourists in your city?
5 Where are your mom and dad from?

4 **TASK** **Write about a town or a city.**

• Choose a town or city and write a description of it. Use the first paragraph in the text and these phrases to help you.
 It's in the north / east ... of ... It's a ... city.
 It's on the ... River. It has ... There is / are ...
• Read your text to the class, but don't say the name of the town or city.
• The other students guess your town or city.

CULTURE ● The English-speaking world

I can talk and write about languages in my country.

1 ● 1.45 **Answer the questions about the countries in the box.
Then read and listen to the text and check your answers.**

Japan   Australia   Poland   the United Kingdom   the U.S.   India   China   South Africa   Brazil

1   In which of these countries is English a first language?
2   In which of these countries do people speak English as an official language?
3   In which of these countries do people speak English as a foreign language?

Are you speaking English?

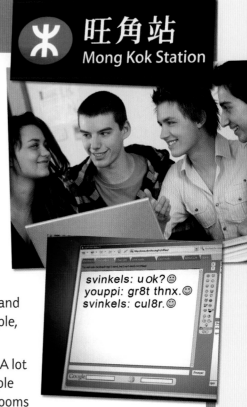

旺角站
Mong Kok Station

svinkels: u ok?☺
youppi: gr8t thnx.☺
svinkels: cul8r.☺

In countries like the United Kingdom, the U.S., and Australia, people speak English as a first language. But they don't speak exactly the same English. English sounds different in these countries because people use different pronunciation and there are different words for some things. The British don't say "soccer", they say "football", and they say "film", not "movie". Some Australians say "G'day", not "Hi", and they don't say "this afternoon", they say "this arvo". In some countries, for example India and some African countries, there are a lot of different languages, so people use English as the official language.

In countries where English isn't a first language, people speak English as a foreign language. People want to study English because it's an international language; it's in movies, magazines, and pop songs. A lot of people, especially scientists and business people, use English when they work, travel, or use a computer.

About 80 percent of the information on the Internet is in English. A lot of people communicate on the Internet in English, too. Some people write a different type of English when they communicate in chat rooms or by instant messages like MSN. They use words like "uok?", "thnx", and "cul8r". These words are faster to write than "Are you OK?", "Thanks", and "See you later"!

2 **Read the text again and answer the questions.**

1   Do people in the U.S. and Britain speak the same English? Why / Why not?
2   What do some Australians say when they meet someone?
3   Why do some countries use English as an official language?
4   Why do people want to learn English?
5   Why do people use shorter words in messages?
6   What does "cul8r" mean?

3 **YOUR CULTURE** **Answer the questions.**

1   What is the official language in your country? Is there more than one?
2   What other languages do people speak in your country? Where?
3   Do people use different pronunciation in different parts of your country? Where?
4   What foreign languages do students usually learn in schools? Why?

4 **TASK** **Write about languages in your country.**

•   Look at your answers in exercise 3 and write a short paragraph for each question.
•   Exchange texts with another student and correct any language and spelling mistakes.

CULTURE ■ National parks

I can write about national parks in my country.

1 ● 2.16 Look at the pictures and answer the questions about a national park. Then read and listen to the text and check your answers.

1 Where is this national park?
2 What other animals do you think live in the park?

2 Read the text again and answer the questions.

1 How old is Banff National Park?
2 How big is the park?
3 What endangered animal lives in the park?
4 How many people visit the park every year?
5 When can you see wolves?
6 What animal is dangerous on the road?

THE GREAT OUTDOORS

Where can you see wild bears and elks in their natural environment? Where are wolves and mountain goats safe from hunters? Created in 1885, Banff National Park is Canada's first national park and the home of many wild animals.

Banff National Park is in the north of the Rocky Mountains, in the west of Canada. There are 6,641 square kilometers of beautiful mountains, forests, rivers, and lakes in the park. This is home for fifty-three different mammals and hundreds of birds, fish, and amphibians. Some of these animals are very rare, for example the endangered mountain lion. But others, like elk or bighorn sheep, are common. You can often see these animals from your car when you are driving in the park!

The park is a great tourist attraction and over four and a half million people visit it every year. One very popular animal is the wolf. About forty wolves live in the park today and many people come to see them. But it's very difficult to see wolves because they are scared of people and they only hunt at night.

When you are walking or driving in the park, you need to be very careful because some animals are dangerous. Every year, there are road accidents with elks. In spring, male elks sometimes attack cars! Bears don't usually attack people. They can't see very well, but they run away if they hear people.

There are forty-two national parks in Canada, but they only cover 2.5 percent of the country. This is a very small area for a very big country!

elk

wolf

grizzly bear

3 YOUR CULTURE Answer the questions.

1 What national parks are there in your country?
2 Where are these parks and how big are they?
3 What animals can you see in these parks?
4 Are there any endangered animals?

4 TASK Write about a national park in your country.

• Work in pairs and choose a national park.
• Use the text above and your answers in exercise 3 to help you.
• Write a description of your park.

CULTURE ■ Home schooling

I can discuss the advantages and disadvantages of home schooling.

1 ⬤ 2.31 **Look at the pictures below and answer the questions. Then read and listen to the text and check your answers.**

1 Where is Ella?
2 What is she doing?

MY MOM IS MY TEACHER

It's 9:30 on Tuesday morning and I'm studying, but I'm not at school. That's because I'm home educated. All children in the U.S. must have an education until they are fourteen, in some states eighteen. This is usually at school, but it can be at home. School's boring for me because the classes are really easy, so I stay at home and my mom teaches me.

I study the same subjects as students at school, but I can learn at my level. I'm really good at math and I'm taking high school level math courses. Most students do that when they're sixteen, but I'm only twelve.

I usually study for five hours a day. I don't wear a uniform; I can work in my pajamas if I want! There's a computer in my "classroom" and I do a lot of work on CD-ROMs and the Internet. I have piano practice every day and I play the violin in an orchestra once a week.

I love learning at home. I don't have any brothers and sisters, but I'm never lonely. I go to a community center on the weekends and I have lots of friends. I can talk to other people like me on the computer.

2 **Read the text again and answer the questions.**

1 Why doesn't Ella go to school?
2 What is different about Ella's education compared to students her age at school?
3 What does Ella do when she isn't studying?
4 How does Ella make friends?
5 In your opinion, is Ella's life interesting? Why / Why not?

3 **YOUR CULTURE** **Answer the questions.**

1 When do children usually start school in your country?
2 When can you leave school?
3 Can children be home educated?

4 **TASK** **Have a group debate about the question:** *What is better, home schooling or going to a school?*

• Work in pairs and list the positive and negative things about home schooling and going to a school.
• Join another pair and discuss in your group. Use some of the expressions in the box.

> Home schooling is a good / bad idea because … .
> I think … is great / boring … because … .
> It's good / bad for students to … .
> It's better because … .
> I don't think home schooling is … .

• Compare your ideas with other groups.

CULTURE ■ Roman Britain

I can write about the previous societies in my country.

1 🔊 2.46 **Read and listen to the text. What do we call the Roman cities *Londinium*, *Mamucium*, and *Eboracum* today?**

2 **Read the text again and answer the questions.**

1 What was the Roman name for Britain?
2 Why do we use Julius Caesar's name for the seventh month?
3 Were there many towns and cities in Britain before Roman times?
4 Which city in Britain has a Roman festival every year? Why?
5 Where in Britain can you visit Roman baths?
6 What do modern roads follow?

3 **YOUR CULTURE** **Answer the questions.**

1 What cultures or societies existed in your country 500–1000 years ago?
2 Are there many words from those languages in your language? Do you know any examples?
3 Was there a different name for the town where you live? What was its name?
4 Is there anything in your country from 500 years ago?

4 **TASK** **Write about the previous societies in your country.**

• Before the class, find out about the other cultures in your country – dates, cities, buildings, names.
• In pairs, write a paragraph about this society in your country. Use the text below as a model.

Britannia

The Romans invaded Britain over 2,000 years ago. They called the country *Britannia* and stayed for about 400 years. The Romans changed a lot of things in the country, and we can see the changes in British life today.

Some English words come from the Roman language, Latin, for example *autumn*, *habitat*, and *alien*. The Roman emperor Julius Caesar started today's calendar. Later, they used his name for the seventh month, July, because he was born in that month.

There weren't many towns in Britain before the Roman invasion, and the Romans started a lot of new cities and towns. We live in these cities now, but we call them different names; Roman *Londinium* is now London and *Mamucium* is Manchester. York was a very important town in Roman times. They called it *Eboracum*. Today, people in this city have a Roman festival every year to celebrate their Roman history.

The Romans liked taking baths, and there were public baths in some of the cities. You can visit the Roman baths today – in Bath! The Romans also invented roads, and modern roads in Britain follow the old Roman roads in a lot of places.

Reach Out Options

CULTURE ● **America's favorite games**
I can play a language game in English.

7

1 🔘 3.12 Match the types of games in the box with pictures 1–3. Then read and listen to the text and find the names of the games in the pictures.

> card game   language game   board game

BORED WITH COMPUTER GAMES...?

It's the weekend, and it's raining. How do children in the U.S. spend their free time? Playing computer games, maybe? But what games did they play before computer games?

In the past, people played a lot of card games. One popular game was *Crazy Eights*. In this game, players took turns to put cards on the table. The winner was the first person to finish all of his / her cards. Children liked games like *Crazy Eights* because they were fun and easy.

Board games were also very popular in the U.S. Younger children liked simple games such as *Snakes and Ladders*. You go up the board when you land on a ladder and down when you land on a snake. The first player to get to the top of the board is the winner. Older children liked strategy games like *Monopoly*. Players travel around the board, buy houses and hotels, and make money.

American people loved language games, too, such as *Hangman*. In *Hangman*, one player thinks of a word, and the other player guesses letters in the word. *Scrabble* was another popular language game, and it's still popular today.

Today, you can play *Monopoly*, *Scrabble*, and other traditional games on the computer. But why not turn your computer off and play a real game with your friends this weekend? It's more fun!

2 Read the text again and answer the questions.
1 How do children in the U.S. spend their free time now?
2 What do you need to play *Crazy Eights*?
3 Is *Snakes and Ladders* a difficult game?
4 What do you do in *Monopoly*?
5 What type of game is *Hangman*?

3 YOUR CULTURE Answer the questions.
1 What games did people play in your country before TV and computers?
2 Do you sometimes play *Hangman*, *Monopoly*, or *Scrabble*?
3 What board games are popular in your country?
4 What do you usually do in your free time?

4 TASK Play a language game.
- Work in small groups and read the rules of the game.
- Play the game in your group. If necessary, correct other players' sentences.
- The first group to finish is the winner.

Rules

Players take turns making sentences. The first sentence starts with the letter A (**A**re you late?). The second sentence starts with the letter B (**B**ig cars are expensive.) Continue like this to the letter Z.

You can make questions and affirmative, negative, and imperative sentences. You can start a sentence with the name of a place or a person if you're stuck. You can't miss your turn or make incorrect sentences.

CULTURE ■ Famous explorers
I can understand a text about a famous explorer.

On top of the world

Mount Everest in the Himalayas is every climber's dream. The 8,850-meter mountain is the highest place in the world and a very dangerous mountain. The weather changes all the time and it is often very windy and cold.

In the early 20th century, other expeditions tried to climb Everest but failed, and many people died there. Finally, on May 29, 1953, Edmund Hillary from New Zealand and Tenzing Norgay from Nepal became the first people to stand on the summit of Mount Everest.

Edmund Hillary was born in Auckland in New Zealand. He wasn't a very athletic young person, but he liked climbing and he had a dream. "Someday I'm going to climb Everest," he told a friend. He was serious, but nobody believed him! In those days, people didn't know if it was possible to climb higher than 8,000 meters because there isn't a lot of oxygen.

When he was 33, Hillary joined a British expedition to climb Everest. At 6:30 a.m. on May 29, Hillary and Norgay left their camp at 8,503 meters and started climbing. They both carried heavy oxygen bottles. They were lucky because the weather was good. Five hours later, at 11:30 a.m., they were on top of the world! They spent fifteen minutes on the summit of Everest and Hillary took a photo of Norgay, but he didn't take a photo of himself! The news of their climb was in all the newspapers, and the two men were heroes before they arrived home.

1 🔊 3.26 **Look at the pictures and answer the questions. Then read and listen to the text and check your answers.**

1 What mountain are the people climbing?
2 Do you know who these climbers are?

2 Read the text again and answer the questions.

1 What is the weather like on Mount Everest?
2 What was Edmund Hillary's dream when he was young?
3 Why is it dangerous to go higher than 8,000 meters?
4 What did Hillary and Norgay take with them on the climb?
5 Why were Hillary and Norgay lucky?
6 Who is in the picture on the summit of Everest?

3 YOUR CULTURE Answer the questions.

1 What famous explorers or adventurers are / were from your country?
2 Where did they go and how did they travel?
3 What did they do? Why was their adventure special?
4 What explorer(s) in the world do you admire? Why?
5 Would you like to be an explorer or an adventurer?

4 TASK Planning and asking about an expedition.

- Work in pairs and imagine you are going on an expedition to an extreme place (North / South Pole, Sahara Desert, Matterhorn Mountain, Congo River, Mars, etc.).
- Make notes about dates, route, transportation, weather, languages, dangers, etc. Make a list of things to take with you.
- Ask and answer Yes / No questions with another pair. Guess where they are going.

Are you going to wear... ?

Are you going to travel by ... ?

Are you going to speak ... ?

1 Complete the puzzle with free time words.
What's the mystery word in gray?

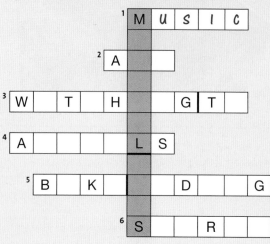

¹ M U S I C
² A
³ W T H G T
⁴ A L S
⁵ B K D G
⁶ S R

Mystery word: _____

2 Follow the lines and complete the sentences.

Joe is into **watching** TV.

1 Rosa is crazy about ___.
2 Penny is interested in ___.
3 Mark is interested in ___.
4 Chris is really into ___.
5 David prefers ___.

Joe　　① Rosa　　② Penny　　③ Mark　　④ Chris　　⑤ David

3 Spot the difference. Look at the two pictures of Sally and Pete in class. Write the things that are different in picture 2.

Sally has a small bag.

VOCABULARY PUZZLES ◼ Places in a town • Describing places

Mystery word: _____

1 Look at the map and complete the puzzle with the names of the places you can see. What's the mystery word in gray?

2 Use the code to write the adjectives.

A	B	C	D	E	F	G	H	I	J	K	L	M
◆	✪	☆	✳	♥	✿	❖	➡	♠	✏	✈	☎	✚

N	O	P	Q	R	S	T	U	V	W	X	Y	Z
➤	♣	☙	✳	✝	⊠	▲	◗	★	●	➽	❭	↕

✳ ◗ ♠ ♥ ▲   *quiet*

1 ✿ ✝ ♠ ♥ ➤ ✳ ☎ ❭
2 ♣ ☎ ✳
3 ◗ ❖ ☎ ❭
4 ⊠ ◆ ✿ ♥
5 ✳ ♠ ✝ ▲ ❭

3 Complete the puzzle with the opposites of the adjectives from exercise 2.

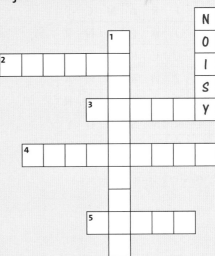

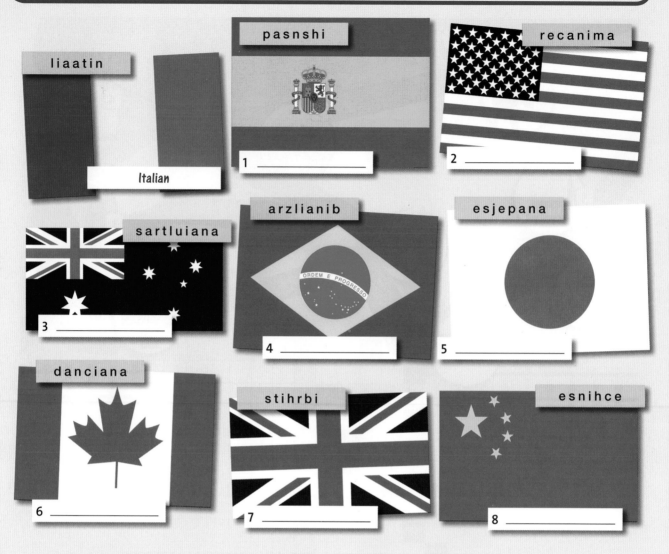

liaatin

Italian

pasnshi

1 _____

recanima

2 _____

sartluiana

3 _____

arzlianib

ORDEM E PROGRESSO

4 _____

esjepana

5 _____

danciana

6 _____

stihrbi

7 _____

esnihce

8 _____

1 Look at the flags and write the nationality.

2 Find eight more countries. Use the gray letters to spell one more country.

P	O	L	A	N	D	A	G
Y	B	F	R	A	N	C	E
S	R	J	A	P	A	N	R
P	A	L	C	K	I	T	M
A	Z	Z	H	R	P	H	A
I	I	Q	I	T	F	E	N
N	L	R	N	S	J	U	Y
C	A	N	A	D	A	K	L

The mystery country is: ___.

3 Find five routines in the puzzles. Write the words below.

F	I	K
S	I	
O	H	
N	W	R

1
A	T	W
H	V	
C	T	

2
O	B	O
D		E
T		G

3
U	H	N
C	L	
V	H	
A	E	

4
S	A	T
W	O	
R	T	
K	R	

5
G	E
P	U
T	

finish work

1 Read the clues and complete the puzzle.

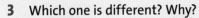
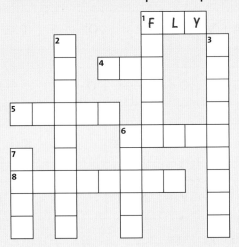

ACROSS
1 A small black insect – most people don't like them!
4 A night bird with big eyes.
5 It has two legs and it's the most dangerous "animal" of them all!
6 A long, thin reptile with no legs.
8 A very big gray animal with a long nose.

DOWN
1 A big bird – it flies in the sky and hunts small animals.
2 A very smart reptile – it can change color.
3 A beautiful insect – it flies from flower to flower.
6 A large ocean fish with very big teeth!
7 A big animal with four legs – it's often black or brown. It sometimes catches fish in the river.

2 Complete the puzzle with animal behavior verbs. What's the mystery animal in gray?

The mystery animal is: ___

3 Which one is different? Why?

The frog is different because it doesn't fly.

1 _____

2 _____

3 _____

4 _____

5 _____

VOCABULARY PUZZLES ■ Activities in and out of school • Food and drink **5**

1 Use the code to write the activities.

A	B	C	D	E	F	G	H	I	J	K	L	M
◆	✪	☆	✳	♥	❀	✧	⊶	♠	✏	✈	☎	✚

N	O	P	Q	R	S	T	U	V	W	X	Y	Z
➤	♣	🍎	✴	✢	✉	▲	◗	★	●	➡	❭	↕

✚◆▲⊶ math

1 ✉☆♠♥➤☆♥

2 ✳◆➤☆♥

3 ⊶♠✉▲♣✢❭

4 ☆⊶♥✉✉

5 ✉♣☆☆♥✢

6 ✧♥♣✴✧✢◆🍎⊶❭

7 ✳✢◆✧◆

2 Order the letters and write the secret message.

A	V	E			2		O'			S	T		

G	E	O			C	L	O			I		H	

		T	E			A			C	K.			

P	H	Y			A	T			G	R	A		

Message: *I have* _____

3 Spot the difference. Write affirmative or negative sentences about picture 2 with food and drink words and *some* or *any*.

In picture 2 …
There aren't any vegetables.
There are some apples.
There isn't any fruit juice.

VOCABULARY PUZZLES ■ Jobs • Regular verbs

1 Find eight words for people. Use the yellow letters to spell a job.

K	I	N	G	H	W	R	I	T	E	R
I	J	F	W	E	P	L	N	Q	W	M
D	K	S	V	X	E	A	Q	U	Z	U
O	N	L	R	P	Z	H	V	E	T	S
C	Z	B	G	L	N	B	S	E	J	I
T	A	C	T	O	R	K	G	N	P	C
O	W	Z	T	R	F	I	U	T	E	I
R	I	N	V	E	N	T	O	R	X	A
C	X	M	A	R	T	I	S	T	Q	N

The yellow word is _____.

2 Follow the lines and match the people with the things they used for their job. Write the jobs.

Picasso was an artist.

3 Find six regular verbs. Use each letter once. Then write the simple past forms.

A A A	C C̷	V V V
E E E	G	H
I	N N N	O Ø
R R	S S̷	T T

c r o s s   crossed
1 i _ _ a d _
2 _ _ _ _ e l
3 n _ m _
4 i _ _ e _ _
5 c _ _ n _ _
6 d _ _ _ _ v e _

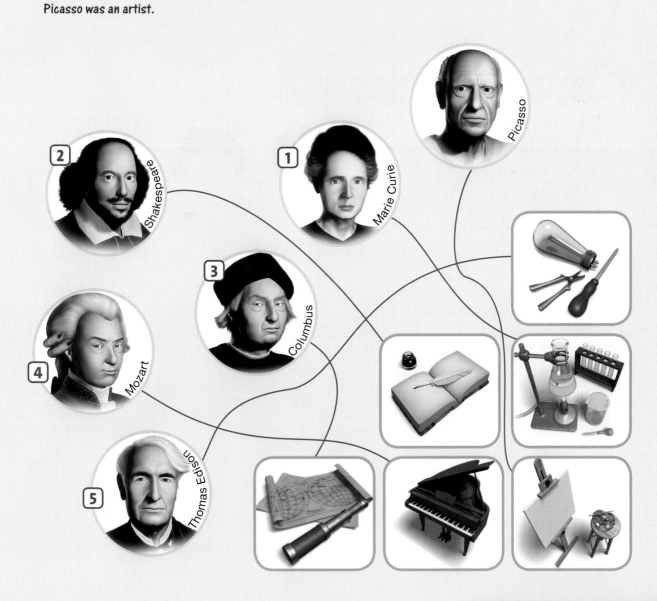

1 Complete the puzzle. Write the simple past forms of the words in the box.

> become   eat   go   have   ~~lose~~   make
> meet   write   know   win   sell   take

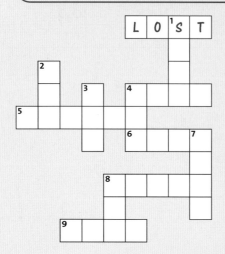

3 Write the simple past form of the missing verbs in the puzzle. Then use the letters in the blue boxes to make a mystery word.

1 I ___ part in a competition.
2 He ___ the race today.
3 I ___ my friend at table tennis.
4 You ___ a goal.
5 We ___ a 800 meter race.
6 She ___ a famous tennis player.
7 They ___ to the soccer game in Mexico City.

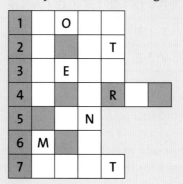

Mystery sports word: ___

2 Complete the table. Look at the pictures and use the letters in the box. Use each letter only once.

G	R	F	D	M
R	H	T	N	
C	A	S	U	C
H	K	E	R	A
U	E	O	T	Y	L
R	S	E	T	A

		G	R	E	E	N	
	eye color	G	R	E	E	N	
1	hair color						
2	hair						
3	other features						
4	build						
5	height						

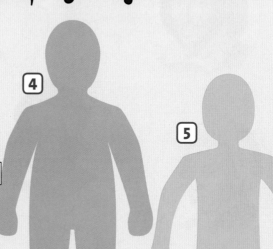

1 Which pieces of expedition equipment can you find in the rainforest?

1 flashlight

① gfhstlalih

② ascmops

③ nersecsnu

④ secnit pereletn

⑤ pma

⑥ vesot

⑦ trsif dia tki

⑧ cakbacpk

⑨ entt

⑩ frpowetrao htesloc

2 What's the weather like in the United States? Unscramble the letters. Label the map.

1 gofyg   *foggy*
2 niayr
3 wnyso
4 cyi
5 dolc
6 uynsn
7 tho
8 mtrsyo

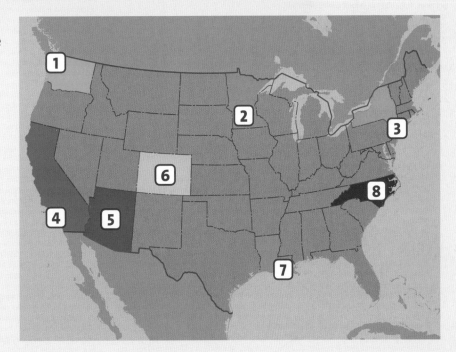

ACKNOWLEDGMENTS

The publisher would like to thank the following for permission to reproduce photographs
and video footage: Alamy Images; Amnesty; CERN; Corbis; Getty Images; Google; MK2;
NASA; Photolibrary; POST; Rex Features; The United Nations; The Wellcome Trust; Zooid

The publisher and authors would like to thank the following teachers for their
contribution to the development of this course: Romaine Ançay, Ursula Bader, Dominique
Baillifard, Kinga Belley, Jaantje Bodt, Michel Bonvin, Coralie Clerc, Teresita Curbelo, Yvona
Doležalová, Lukas Drbout, Pierre Filliez, Olga Forstová, Christelle Fraix, Attie van Grieken,
Roger Grünblatt, Çağrı Güngörmüş, Christoph Handschin, Joe Hediger, Jana Vacková
Hezinová, Maria Higina, Jaroslava Jůzková, Martin Kadlec, Urs Kalberer, Lena Kigouk, Joy
Kocher, Murat Kotan, Marcela Kovářová, Jitka Kremínová, Lucie Macháčková, Doubravka
Matulová, Jitka Melounková, Dana Mikešová, Noémi Nikolics, Sabrina Ragno, Denis
Richon, Sonja Rijkse, Susanna Schwab, Dagmar Šimková, Jana Šimková, Nuria Smyth,
Lenka Špačková, Rita Steiner, Anne-Marie Studer, Milan Svoboda, Anneli Terre-Blanche,
Maria Cecilia Verga, Marta Vergara, Donna Van Wely.

*The publisher and authors would like to extend special thanks to Ursula Schaer for sharing her insights
and for the material she contributed to this book.*

*The publisher and authors would like to thank Sue Sileci for her valuable work in developing
Reach Out.*

Illustrations by: Mark Draisey p.4, 14, 16, 22, 41, 112; KJA artists p.29, 95, 101, 103; Dave
Oakley/Arnos Design Ltd p.95 (weather symbols); Andy Parker p.19, 58, 72, 73, 75, 94, 101,
117; Gregory Roberts/Sylvie Poggio p.90, 112, 113, 119; Oxford Designers & Illustrators
p.95, 105, 113 (school, apartment building), 119 (map); Stephanie Strickand/Sylvie Poggio
p.100.

Commissioned photography by: Chris King p.14, 24, 44, 52.

Cover photographs: Getty (students/Ken Kaminesky), iStockphoto (Hikers/Sergiy Zavgorodny),
(Friends taking photo/Damir Cudic); PunchStock (Teen girls listening to music/Photodisc).

The publisher would like to thank the following for their permission to reproduce photographs:
AKGImages pp.6 (Margherita, Queen (Humbert I) of Italy, born Princess of Savoy-Genoa;
Turin 20.11.1851-Bordighera 4.1.1926.-Portrait.-Photo, colorised after the drawing by
Michele Gordigiani (1830–1909). Rome, Palazzo del Quirinale.), 59 (Antoine Sax),
59 (Margherita, Queen (Humbert I) of Italy, born Princess of Savoy-Genoa; Turin
20.11.1851-Bordighera 4.1.1926.-Portrait.-Photo, colorised after the drawing by Michele
Gordigiani (1830–1909). Rome, Palazzo del Quirinale.); Alamy Images pp.6 (Manhattan/Clive
Sawyer), 6 (Exeter Academy/Susan Pease), 9 (Teenage girls talking/Mia Caruana), 9 (boy
reading/Picture Partners), 9 (Football game/blickwinkel), 9 (teen painting/Mike Booth),
10 (Boy holding skateboard/Arco Images GmbH), 11 (London skyline/JLImages), 11 (Boy
jumps on skateboard/Paul Kuroda), 12 (ZUMA Wire Service), 15 (Student with laptop/
PictureNet Corporation), 20 (Dubai mall/travelstock44), 22 (Brighton/John Boud), 29 (Ginza,
Tokyo/Chad Ehlers), 29 (Barges in Rhine Valley/Germany Images David Crossland), 29 (Pizza/
David Ball), 29 (Antique globe/MichaelXuereb.com), 29 (Fish and chip sign on beach/Geraint
Lewis), 30 (Manhattan/Clive Sawyer), 30 (Chinatown/Peter Horree), 31 (Preparing pasta/
Danny Clifford), 32 (Child labour at shoe factory/Des Willie), 32 (Chinese schoolgirl/Mark
Henley/Imagestate Media Partners Limited - Impact Photos), 43 (Sightseers watching seals/
Alan Spencer Norfolk), 47 (Great White Shark/Malcolm Schuyl), 47 (Humpback whale/
Stephen Frink Collection), 50 (Exeter Academy/Susan Pease), 50 (Boys/Bob Daemmrich), 54 (Picture
Partners), 57 (art students/Photofusion Picture Library), 59 (Levi Strauss/Pictorial Press Ltd),
59 (Levi Jeans red tag/PSL Images), 59 (Marie Curie 1910/Mary Evans Picture Library),
59 (Periodic table of elements/WidStock), 59 (Dr Martens boot display/Malcolm Freeman),
60 (Jaguar/Motoring Picture Library), 61 (William Shakespeare/Classic Image), 61 (Margaret
Adelaide of Savoy/The Print Collector), 62 (Hell, Michigan sign/Jim West), 63 (Lorgues 4
Voyages map/Mary Evans Picture Library), 65 (Brian Jannsen), 67 (Charles river/David R.
Frazier Photolibrary, Inc.), 67 (Coffee shop/Kim Karpeles), 69 (Ice Hockey player/Stefan
Sollfors), 80 (Bird watching/David Tipling), 80 (Rainforest campsite/mediacolor's),
81 (Highway/Joe Sohm/Visions of America, LLC), 83 (Graduates/Andrew Fox), 87 (Camping/
Scottish Viewpoint), 87 (Mountain climber in tent/StockShot), 91 (Hip Hop men dancing/
Gino's Premium Images), 94 (teenagers/Kuttig-People-2), 104 (Surfer/Doug Steley B),
105 (JoeFox), 108 (mother & daughter/Brownstock Inc.), 110 (Eric Fowke), 110 (scrabble tiles/
Paul Bradforth), 111 (Tenzing Norgay and Edmund Hillary/Royal Geographic Society); Ardea
p.99 (lion fish/Jean Michel Labat); Arnos Design Ltd pp.11 (History of Art book),
13 (Computer/Dave Oakley), 53 (food face), 79 (Sleeping bag/Dave Oakley), 79 (Waterproof
jacket & trousers/Dave Oakley), 79 (Map/Dave Oakley), 79 (Suncream/Dave Oakley),
79 (Insect repellent/Dave Oakley); Bridgeman Art Library Ltd pp.8 (Harvest in Provence,
June 1888 (oil on canvas), Gogh, Vincent van (1853–90)/The Israel Museum, Jerusalem,
Israel/Gift of Yad Hanadiv, Jerusalem, from the collection of Miriam Alexandrine de
Rothschild), 53 (Arcimboldo, Giuseppe (1527–93)/Private Collection Agnew's, London, UK),
69 (Panathenaic black figure amphora depicting a foot race (pottery), Greek, (5th century
BC)/Musee Municipal Antoine Vivenel, Compiegne, France/Lauros/Giraudon), The Bridgeman
Art Library Lauros/Giraudon), 96 (Poplars, 1891 (oil on canvas), Monet, Claude (1840–1926)/
Fitzwilliam Museum, University of Cambridge, UK), 96 (Harvest in Provence, June 1888 (oil on
canvas), Gogh, Vincent van (1853–90)/The Israel Museum, Jerusalem, Israel/Gift of Yad
Hanadiv, Jerusalem, from the collection of Miriam Alexandrine de Rothschild), 96 (The
Poppies, Henry, George F. (1858–1943)/© City of Edinburgh Museums and Art Galleries,
Scotland); Corbis pp.6 (explorer/Paul A. Souders), 9 (boy on bike/Ocean), 9 (chatting online/
Fancy), 9 (girl with dog/Estelle Klawitte/zefa), 22 (Miami/Dennis Degnan), 23 (Unalaska/
Brooks Kraft), 30 (Students/Tetra Images), 32 (Teenager eating lunch with family/Caterina
Bernardi), 32 (Teenager doing homework/Ted Horowitz), 34 (Moxie Productions/Blend
Images), 59 (Alfred Nobel/Bettmann), 59 (Nobel prize/Ted Spiegel), 59 (Amerigo Vespucci/
Stefano Bianchetti), 60 (Canon camera/Yuriko Nakao), 61 (The Beatles/Michael Ochs
Archive), 74 (Ocean), 82 (Fog/Alistair Baker), 82 (Icicles/Fancy), 82 (Explorer/PaulA. Souders),
84 (Per Magnus Persson/Johnr Imag), 85 (Camping/Stuart Westmoreland), 85 (Kayaking/
Henrik Trygg), 98 (angry person/Left Lane Productions), 99 (snake/Martin Harvey),
105 (Ocean), 108 (friends playing/MM Productions/image100); Douglas Sefert p.42 (fish
feeding); Dreamstime pp.79 (Portable stove/Timrobbins), 79 (First aid kit/Webking),
79 (Compass/Iofoto); Education Photos pp.49 (drama/John Walmsley); Getty Images
pp.6 (soccer/Erik Isakson), 9 (taking photo/altrendo images), 9 (Martial arts/Andy Crawford/
Dorling Kindersley), 9 (girls playing video games/Britt Erlanson/Stone), 10 (Teenage girl on
athletic field/Matt Henry Gunther/Taxi Japan), 10 (soccer/Erik Isakson), 12 (Teenage couple
reading/Leon/Riser), 13 (Roger Federer/AFP), 20 (The Burj Dubai/Bloomberg via Getty
Images), 23 (Mexico City/Panoramic Images), 25 (VisionsofAmerica/Joe Sohm), 27 (Girls in
football kit/Alistair Berg/Taxi), 35 (Canadian flag outside Parliament Buildings/Kevin Miller/
Stone), 47 (Saltwater crocodile/Sam Abell/National Geographic), 55 (Thomas Barwick),
60 (Noah Graham/NBAE), 61 (Chemists Pierre and Marie Curie/Time & Life Pictures),
64 (Yellow Dog Productions), 67 (Widener library/Steve Dunwell), 69 (World Cup.1966:
Brazil V Hungary/Time & Life Pictures), 69 (Olympic swimmers/Sports Illustrated), 69 (NFL
game/Sports Illustrated), 69 (Skateboarder Andy McDonald), 77 (Santa Maria ship/Bernard
Van Berg/The Image Bank), 80 (Family in boat/Brian Bailey/The Image Bank), 82 (Snow on
house/Penny Kendall), 82 (Rain on window/Arctic-Images), 82 (Lightning/Valentin Casarsa),
93 (Couple picking fruit/Cultura/Liam Norris), 98 (happy woman/LWA/Taxi), 98 (confused
man/Taizan Kamijo), 98 (conversation/Leon/Riser), 98 (thumbs-up/Andy Sacks/The Image
Bank), 107 (Banff National Park/Max Bolotnikov/Photographer's Choice), 107 (Red stag/Tim
Flach/Stone), 107 (Wolves/Paul Oomen/Photographer's Choice), 107 (Brown bear runs
through water/Jami Tarris/Botanica), 110 (monopoly/Bruno Vincent), 111 (Mount Everest),
111 (Norgay Tenzing On Mount Everest/Hulton Archive), cover (College students/Ken
Kaminesky/Brand X Pictures); Image Quest Marine pp.39 (whale/James D. Watt), 39 (tiger
shark/Roger Steene), 39 (snake/Jez Tryner), 39 (Owl butterfly wing/Chris Parks),
39 (crocodile/Mark Conlin); iStockphoto pp.11 (DVD case/zoomstudio), 13 (elephant/Prill
Mediendesign & Fotografie), 17 (books/Andrzej Tokarski), 17 (LCD TV/ronen), 37 (map of
Australia/shimura), 37 (Bondi beach/EddWestmacott), 42 (Beaver building dam/Jeffrey
Hochstrasser), 49 (laptop/T Cstin), 49 (maths/Maria Maciuca), 49 (chess/bluestocking),
49 (paint palette/Gino Santa Maria), 49 (science/Pali Rao), 49 (geography/Marcelo Wain),
57 (modern building/Ian Jeffery), 57 (Teenagers in class/Richard Bowden), 57 (salad/doram),
59 (saxophone/Barry Gregg), 59 (USA flag/ayzek), 79 (Torch/Chris Elwell), 82 (Sun/Stefanie
Timmermann), 106 (Students with laptop/Dean Mitchell), cover (Hikers/Sergiy Zavgorodny),
cover (Friends taking photo/Damir Cudic); Keith Meadley p.109 (Roman festival, York);
Kobal Collection pp.13 (Casino Royale (2006)/Eon/Danjaq/Sony), 77 (Spiderman/Columbia/
Marvel), 93 (Indiana Jones and the Kingdom of the Crystal Skull/Lucasfilm/Paramount Pictures),
93 (Scream/Miramax), 93 (Avatar/Twentieth Century-Fox Film Corporation), 93 (Ace Ventura
Pet Detective/Morgan Creek International); Manuel Presti p.42 (falcon attacking birds); Mary
Evans Picture Library pp.69 (First Tour de France, 1903/Rue des Archives/Tallandier),
69 (Windsor Real Tennis 1500/Illustrated London News Ltd); Michael Ging p.62 (Why road
sign, Arizona/Michael Ging); Nature Picture Library pp.6 (killer whales/Brandon Cole),
42 (chameleon catching insect/Kim Taylor), 42 (bear catching salmon/Eric Baccega),
45 (killer whales/Brandon Cole), 80 (Emerald tree boa/Pete Oxford), 80 (Squirrel monkey/
Pete Oxford), 99 (blue poison arrow frog/Ingo Arndt); Nintendo p.63 (Super Mario), 70 (The
Sims screenshot), 70 (Super Mario on DS); Oxford University Press pp.7 (Golfer/Brand X
Pictures), 17 (girl/Photodisc), 17 (Dog/Photodisc), 17 (snowboarding/Digital Vision),
17 (guitar/Photodisc), 17 (mobile phone/D. Hurst), 37 (Sydney harbour/Photodisc),
37 (Sydney Harbour Bridge/Stockbyte), 45 (Polar bear/Digital Vision), 91 (Cinema ticket roll/
Stockbyte), 99 (parrot/Stockdisc), 99 (mouse/Photodisc), 109 (Roman Baths/Digital Vision);
Panos Pictures p.40 (ivory/Betty Press); Photolibrary pp.8 (Girl listening to music/Comstock),
27 (Boy holding digital camera/Jack Hollingsworth/White), 39 (Brown bear/David Tipling/
White), 42 (Bird feeding young/White), 42 (Dolphins jumping near boat/Image Source),
49 (Boys in football kit/OJO Images), 59 (pizza/Maximilian Stock), 87 (Couple outdoors at
campsite/Monkey Business Images Ltd/Stockbroker), 104 (Looking through binoculars/
Photoalto/Zen Shui), 104 (Girl listening to music/Comstock); Press Association Images
pp.60 (Keira Knightley/Yu Mok), 71 (Jonathan Wendel/Damian Dovarganes/AP), 75 (Maria
Sharapova/Fiona Hanson); PunchStock pp.8 (Generation Y kids hanging out/Photodisc),
9 (girl with headphones/Blend Images), 9 (watching TV/Fuse), 21 (Scenic mountain town/
Tetra Images), 27 (Basketball player/Blend Images), 29 (The White House/National
Geographic), 51 (Mother and child talking/Tetra Images), 79 (Tent/Ryan McVay),
79 (Rucksack/Stockbyte), 88 (teens/Onoky), 88 (Generation Y kids hanging out/Photodisc),
92 (girls ordering/Polka Dot Images), 98 (shocked woman/Polka Dot), 98 (bored woman/
Pixland), 100 (basketball/Brand X Pictures), cover (Teen girls listening to music/Photodisc);
Rex Features pp.13 (Beyonce Knowles/Picture Perfect), 13 (Batman/Warner Bros/Everett),
59 (Dr Klaus Maertens/Nils Jorgensen), 62 (Pray road sign/Jim Pickerell), 67 (Harvard/Spa
Press); Shannon Richardson p.62 (Happy road sign, Michegan); Shutterstock pp.39 (spider/
erlle74), 39 (human eye/ParryPix), 39 (seal/Oleg Nekhaev), 39 (parrot/ivvv1975),
39 (elephant/Jeff Gynane), 91 (Debby Wong).

*Although every effort has been made to trace and contact copyright holders before publication, this has
not been possible in some cases. We apologise for any apparent infringement of copyright and, if notified,
the publisher will be pleased to rectify any errors or omissions at the earliest possible opportunity.*